Over The Hills To Calke

150 years of memories of Calke Abbey and the Harpur-Crewes

Over The Hills To Calke

150 years of memories of Calke Abbey and the Harpur-Crewes

L. J. Cox

First published in Great Britain by
The Breedon Books Publishing Company Limited
45 Friar Gate, Derby DE1 1DA
1989
2nd edition 2000
© L. J. Cox 2000
Published by L. J. Cox,
The Grange,
Twyford, Derby,
DE73 1HJ.

All Rights Reserved. No part of this publication may be reproduced, stored in a retrieval system or transmitted in any form, or by any means, electronic, mechanical, photocopying, recording or otherwise without the prior permission in writing of the Copyright holders, nor be otherwise circulated in any form or binding or cover other than in which it is published and without a similar condition including this condition being imposed on the subsequent publisher

ISBN 0-9539876-0-4

Cover Design and Printed by
Black Bear Press Limited.
King's Hedges Road, Cambridge.

Contents

Chapter One	Early Days	8
Chapter Two	My life on the Estate	27
Chapter Three	Some Favourite Tenants	33
Chapter Four	Calke Abbey	37
Chapter Five	Calke Park	46
Chapter Six	The Gardens	51
Chapter Seven	Camping in the Park	54
Chapter Eight	The Hudsons and Calke	59
Chapter Nine	Hannah Hudson	72
Chapter Ten	The Early History of Calke	78
Chapter Eleven	Harpurs and Harpur Crewes	80
Chapter Twelve	Sir George Crewe	83
Chapter Thirteen	Sir John Crewe	90
Chapter Fourteen	Sir Vauncey Crewe	93
Chapter Fifteen	Mrs. H. E. H. Mosley	104
Chapter Sixteen	The Last Years	108
Chapter Seventeen	Postscript	113
Appendix		115
About the Author		120

*"For is not half our action
prompted by a restless
desire to scan the horizon
and look over the hill-tops?"*

John Buchan
from 'Scholar Gipsies'

ACKNOWLEDGEMENTS

I owe a debt of gratitude to many people, too numerous to mention by name, who have helped me in the preparation of this book and I hope they will accept my thanks expressed through this general acknowledgement.

I must, however, express particular thanks to Miss G. F. Purchas for information concerning her grandfather, the Reverend W. H. Purchas, Mr Howard Colvin for the benefit of his research into the Harpur-Crewe family history, Mr Roy Christian and my sister Kathleen and Sylvia Fox for help and advice, Mrs Patricia Harby for help with photography and last, but not least, my cousin, Phyllis Brown, for help with typing.

The Grange
Twyford
Derbyshire.

Photographs: National Trust, pages 38, 39, 79, 81 and back cover; Derby Evening Telegraph, pages 41, 42, 50; R. Bullock page 17; B. Hall page 25; N. J. Clarke pages 46, 47; R. Pegg pages 48, 62; M. J. Bond pages 56, 57; G. F. Purchas page 75; H. Soar page 92; H. Buckston page 114; John Murray page 95.

DEDICATION

To the memory of my father and mother,
John William and Evelyn Watson Cox.

Author's introduction to the second edition.

Following publication of the first edition in 1989, I have received many requests for further information.

Miss Airmyne Harpur-Crewe was the last member of her family to be associated with Calke Abbey, in direct line from Sir Henry Harpur the first baronet, who arrived there in 1622.

Her death in 1999 seemed the appropriate time to publish this second edition, bringing to a close the story of Calke Abbey and the Harpur-Crewes.

Chapter One
Early Days

UNTIL recent years, few had heard of Calke Abbey, and fewer still had seen the great mansion of the Harpur Crewes, hidden from sight in the valley in Calke Park. In this respect I must claim privilege, having been associated with the Calke Abbey Estate all my life.

I was born at the Smithy Farm, Twyford, part of the Derbyshire Estate some nine miles north of Calke Abbey, where my father was the village blacksmith and a small dairy farmer, farming the thirty six acres of land attached to the blacksmith's shop.

The village of Twyford, alongside the river Trent was then, as now, no more than a hamlet consisting of a few farms and cottages, but in addition to the blacksmith's shop, the village boasted a church dating back at least to Norman times, a Church of England School, and a chain ferry across the river. There used to be a public house called 'The Bell' but this had been pulled down by Sir John Crewe in 1850 when he discovered it had become a rendezvous for poachers. Although a little known place where nothing seems to happen, Twyford has its place in history.

The name means "two fords" and river fords were important when bridges were few and far between. The Romans are reputed to have crossed here. My father remembers one ford in use, by waggons transporting bricks from the Harpur Crewe brickworks at Ticknall.

About the year 700 A.D., St. Guthlac, with his faithful boatman, Tatwin, sailed by. Guthlac, an Anglo Saxon saint, and member of the royal Mercian family, began life as a soldier of fortune in the army of the ancient kingdom of Mercia. Renouncing this life, he became a monk at Repton Priory, but after two years, decided to seek a life of greater solitude in the Fens. His journey along the Trent led to the founding of Croyland Abbey.

In the 17th Century, the major landowners at Twyford were the Harpurs and the Bristowes. During the civil war, the Harpurs were for the king, although the Twyford Harpurs played no active part, whereas Simon Bristowe joined Cromwell's army and killed a Royalist soldier at Tutbury Castle. The soldiers swore to be revenged, and when Simon's brother William died in 1645, his manservant buried him privately at night in Twyford churchyard, and levelled the ground, as the King's army had threatened to come and burn his body.

There had been a ferry at Twyford for many years. One of the earliest references to it was by Viscount Torrington in his Tour of the Midlands in 1790, travelling with his horses, Po and Blacky. On his way to Twyford, he paused to take stock of Sir Robert Burdett's newly erected mansion at nearby Foremark, which he described as "vile architecture in a bad situation". The lake in front, he referred to as a paltry pond with pitiful plantations — "I never wish to enter these Venetian vanities". Describing the ferry crossing he wrote "Po was very quiet in the boat, but Blacky was much alarmed."

Years ago, when someone committed suicide, the ferry boat had a somewhat distressing duty to perform. When to commit suicide was universally regarded as sinful, the body could not be buried in consecrated ground. It had to be buried within the parish, however, usually as far away as possible, near the parish boundary. At Twyford a small part of the parish is on the other side of the river, opposite the village, and suicides were ferried across to be buried in a field called Hailstones. In the church registers, under 6th April 1705, there is an entry in Latin recording that William Smith, a stranger, hanged himself at Twyford and was buried "in a place commonly called Hailstones" (in loc vulgo appellato Hailstones).

The ferry boat belonged to the Harpur Crewe Estate and John Hind, the tenant of Ferry Farm, who had land on both sides of the river, was in charge, and used the boat for access. At Twyford, he practised what must have been a system of dairy farming unique in England.

Each spring, he would drive his cattle along the road to Willington, the next village, to cross the river over the bridge, then back towards home through Repton and Milton to reach his grazing land opposite Twyford village — a journey of 5½ miles to arrive 60 yards away by boat! Each morning and evening throughout the summer, the farm workers would cross the river with buckets, stools and churns to milk the cows in the open air. In the Autumn, the cattle would be brought back by road again, to spend the winter in the cattle sheds at home. The ferry boat is no longer there. Having outlived its main purpose after the tenant of Ferry Farm retired, it was wrecked in the severe floods of 1963.

Twyford Ferry

Milking Time at Ferry Farm.

The Cox family came to Twyford in 1875, having arrived in Derbyshire from Lincolnshire in 1850 when my great great-grandfather John Cox, became bailiff at Swarkeston Lowes Farm, another Harpur Crewe property some three miles from Twyford. His son also John, my great-grandfather, was apprenticed to the Bentleys, Wheelwrights and blacksmiths at Swarkeston and my father was of the third generation of blacksmiths in my family. I remember my great grandfather very well. He died in 1933 aged 97 years. His account books tell us that in his days as the village blacksmith he would mend a bucket for 6d (2½p) and shoe a horse for half a crown (12½p) He made a bicycle in the blacksmiths shop at Twyford and intended to market it, but was beaten by Frank Bowden of Nottingham who did the same thing, and founded the Raleigh Cycle Company. Towards the end of his life, he did however achieve fame, with his photograph in the local papers, standing beside a brussel sprout he had grown, which at 5ft 4ins high was as tall as himself!

When my great-grandfather came to Twyford he took over from the Towle family who had been blacksmiths in the village for several generations. If I had ever had any early ambition, I would have been inspired by one member of that family, William Towle. William, son of Edward Towle the last of blacksmiths, left home to become a page boy at the Midland Hotel in Derby, and through industry and ability rose to become controller of the Midland Railway hotel and catering services.

To him must be given the credit for the introduction of a refreshment service for railway passengers. He arranged for wicker luncheon baskets containing a packed lunch, which could be purchased at the Midland Station in Derby, or St. Pancras in London, the empty basket being left at either station at the end of the journey.

Sir William Towle.

The Smithy Farm at Twyford. John Cox, the author's great-grandfather, is standing outside the blacksmith's shop.

After a distinguished career, he received a knighthood. Throughout his life he never forgot his native village, and was a generous benefactor when Twyford Church was restored after a serious fire in 1910, presenting new oak pews and a stained glass window in memory of his wife. He used to visit us at the Smithy where he was born. I remember him as a very distinguished gentleman, full of old world courtesy and charm, who always kissed my mother's hand in greeting. When he called to see us he always gave me, and my brothers and sister, a brand new ten shilling note (50p) each. This was by far the largest sum of money we were ever given at one time, and nowadays would be worth almost £20. You can imagine we always became excited when Sir William's motor car arrived at the front door. We were of course, never allowed to spend the money. This was always put safely in the bank. In fact our accounts at the Trustee Savings Bank in Derby were opened with the first of those ten shilling notes given to us by Sir William.

During my early years, I attended the tiny Church of England School in the village which had been built in 1843 on land presented to the Church by Sir George Crewe of Calke. Later on when I moved to secondary school in Derby, my fees were paid by the John Harpur Education Foundation, a Twyford charity founded by a member of the Harpur family in the 18th century. Twyford School consisted of a single classroom with an open fire at one end and where all the children from 5 to 11 years of age were taught by Miss Brittan, the only teacher. Numbers were small, the most I remember was twenty two and the smallest number five, of which three were Coxes. Mother used to say at that time that she deserved a medal for keeping the school open. Miss Brittan had to teach all ages, and instruction was on a personal basis.

Morning assembly took the form of a religious service with prayers and hymns. We often sang "All things bright and beautiful" including the third verse, which is now of course politically incorrect.

> The rich man in his castle,
> The poor man at his gate,
> God made them, high or lowly,
> And order'd their estate.

I suppose, if we had thought about it, our rich man in his castle would have been Mrs. Mosley at Calke Abbey, and that gave us no problem.

We always sang grace before mid-day dismissal and again when we re-assembled in the afternoon.

Discipline was strict, and the teaching conducted on lines which I am sure would have been fully approved by Sir George Crewe. There was a tiny school yard but no proper playground and my father, who was one of the school managers, allowed us to use our field in front of the Smithy, which was just across the road from the school. There we played, and sometimes on fine summer days, (and in those days the sun always seemed to shine) classes would be held there under the shade of a large ash tree. Across the field we would often hear the sound of the hammer on the anvil coming from the blacksmiths shop if father happened to working there at the time. If you have ever heard that distinctive sound which will remain with me for all time, you can well imagine how Handel was inspired to write the 'Harmonious Blacksmith' after hearing the blacksmith working in the village of Edgeware in Middlesex.

There were several important days in the school year. On Empire Day we saluted the flag, sang patriotic songs, and Miss Brittan gave a talk on our responsibilities as future citizens of the Empire and all it stood for. Armistice Day was a particularly solemn occasion. We were close in time to the Great War in which relatives and friends of our parents had lost their lives. This day was always observed on the 11th of November, with a religious service and two minutes silence at 11 o'clock.

In those days everything stopped on the hour. Father would cease work in the blacksmith's shop or would halt the horses if he was ploughing the field. I remember how once we were shocked when an uncaring or forgetful motorist drove past the school during the silence. May Day was also celebrated but this had nothing to do with politics. In the morning the boys voted for one of the girls to be May Queen and she was crowned in the afternoon with a wreath of flowers. This was followed by a display of maypole and country dancing to which parents were invited. I can still hear the sound of Sir Roger de Coverley and other country dance tunes coming from that now old fashioned wind up gramophone.

On Shrove Tuesday we always had pancakes, which the mistress made over the open fire in the schoolroom. Miss Brittan supplied the ingredients, and my mother provided the frying pan and other utensils. She did the washing up afterwards, and for this was rewarded with a pancake. As Miss Brittan made each pancake it was shared out among the pupils. She was skilled at pancake tossing but the floor in front of the fireplace was always covered with newspaper in case of a mishap. Pancakes were followed by a half holiday. In fact we seemed to have quite a few extra holidays, half days to

Twyford's Church of England School.

commemorate important church festivals, and others given by the school managers, and by the attendance officer for good attendance.

Every spring, Miss Brittan took us across the river on the ferry boat to visit a cave cut out of rock and known as Anchor Church. It had never been a church, but was once the home of an anchorite or hermit, hence the name. Bluebells grew there in profusion, and the girls were allowed to pick bunches to bring home.

We never went away on holiday so events like this were looked forward to. The highlight of the year was however the school's annual coach trip, usually to the seaside — Skegness, Mablethorpe or Rhyl. We saved up pennies all the year for this trip. I remember one year I was the richest pupil on the coach with ten old pence and being so unused to spending money, brought four pence of this back home.

One morning each week, if the weather was suitable, we would be taken on a nature walk round the parish. In the spring we looked for early flowers and birds nests, noting the progress from. the first laying of eggs in the nests, until the birds flown. Looking for larks' and plover's nests in the open fields and listening to the song of the lark as it rose higher and higher in the clear blue sky, is something I shall always remember. In the same way we observed the farmers working in the fields through the changing seasons, from seedtime to harvest. We did not have to be taught the country code. All that was second nature to us. Farmers worked in harmony with nature, and crops were grown in rotation to preserve fertility. There was no rape of the land. Hedges were never grubbed up to make ever larger prairie like fields, but were carefully cut and laid and trimmed in turn. Autumn fires in the fields were not part of a scorched earth policy but were only the burning of hedge trimmings and weeds during autumn stubble cleaning. Land was kept in permanent pasture or meadow and herb rich meadows were everywhere. The word conservation, now on everyone's lips, was never used. There was conservation all around. It was a world where church spires, not chimneys and cooling towers, dominated the landscape.

Sometimes on these walks round the village, we would be taken into Church where Miss Brittan would show us the Harpur memorials in the Chancel, and the furnishings and their significance. I remember once when we were in the Chancel, being filled with a sense of awe when she told us we must not enter the sanctuary because only the priest was allowed there. One of the highlights of the Church's year was the harvest thanksgiving, the culmination of the year's work on the land. This was held on the last Sunday in September unless the harvest was late, when the festival would be delayed so that we could truthfully sing that all was safely gathered in. The Church was filled with flowers, fruit and vegetables, grown in the parish making a riot of colour, and all this in the days before the professional flower arrangers had perfected their art. Harvest Festival was the one Sunday in the year when there was a service in the evening, and the hanging paraffin lamps were lighted. On the Saturday evening after the lady decorators had departed, I used to go with my father to help him trim the lamps. To take each lamp down he would stand on the pew, having previously placed his cap there to avoid damaging the seat. Having replenished the oil and trimmed the wick, each lamp would be lighted and all allowed to burn for a while to see that everything was in order. I can see now the swinging lamps coming slowly to rest as the operation came to an end.

In those early days, the vicar was the Revd. H.A.Hodges, a versatile gentleman with a white beard. He rode a motor-cycle, and as well as conducting services, could play the organ and was a gifted amateur woodcarver. He made a new pulpit for the church during a restoration scheme following a fire in 1910.

One of his sons, Goderic, was a master at Bedford School where he taught Charles and Henry Jenney (later Harpur Crewe). It was decided that Henry would benefit from extra tuition, so Goderic was invited to stay at Calke during the summer holidays. Henry told me that this had little success because when the time came for lessons, he used to run away, to hide in the park.

Day to day happenings at school, including the pupils' minor misdemeanours were recorded by the mistress in the school log book. Very occasionally she would be late for school herself. She rode a motorcycle and this would sometimes break down. An entry in the log book would read something like this: "My motorcycle broke down this morning and I was late for school, arriving at 9.40 a.m. On arrival I found the children busy at their work'. What she did not know was that we had a lookout standing on a chair, looking through the window towards the village of Willington, to watch for her arrival, so that we could rush to our desks at the last minute to give a good impression! If her arrival was considerably delayed, and we realised that she was going to be absent for the day, the lookout would then transfer to the other side of the schoolroom, to look out in the other direction for the arrival of the replacement, either Mrs. Holmes or Mrs. Palmer from Barrow-on-Trent. This was always a welcome change because discipline under either was less strict. We also had a rather higher opinion of these supply teachers, because they could play the piano with both hands unlike Miss Brittan, who could only pick out the melody with one finger!

Twyford Church.

    Whenever there was an epidemic in the district, Miss Brittan had her own patent method of warding off the disease. On the morning of the chosen day, she would close all the doors and windows, heat a metal dustpan over the fire until it was red hot, then pour on some Jeyes Fluid, which gave off a pungent blue smoke. She then proceeded to walk round the room carrying the smoking dustpan, and we had to take deep breaths of this cleansing vapour. After much coughing and sneezing, the doors and windows were opened, and after the fog had cleared, life returned to normal, and hopefully the pestilence had been kept at bay.

    In school, discipline was strict and bad language so rare as to be virtually non existent. When this did occur however, stern measures were called for . I remember one boy who was foolish enough to have used the word "damn" within the hearing of the mistress, had his tongue washed with carbolic soap and water in front of the whole school, as a warning to us all.

    As a small boy I was regarded as something of a dreamer, and I know this to be true because I distinctly remember, on many occasions during school playtime, standing in the yard holding the railings and looking across to the Foremark hills which interrupted the distant view. To me, at that age, those hills appeared like a range of mountains. I became fascinated, and used to wonder what lay beyond. One day I was to know. At that time I knew vaguely that somewhere over there was Calke Abbey where Mrs. Mosley lived. I knew she owned the whole village where I lived, even the ferry boat on the river, and a good deal more besides, and was highly respected by everyone. Stories were still told about her father, Sir Vauncey, the last of the baronets of Calke, who had died the year after I was born. I also knew that somewhere over there was the village of Ticknall from where a steam traction engine with threshing tackle used to come after harvest, and again in the spring, travelling round the farms to thresh the corn. I remember, as children we were frightened by the traction engine, that monstrous machine belching smoke and steam, and perhaps even more by the formidable character in charge of it. We wondered what sort of a place it was that could produce such a frightening combination of man and machine!

When we were not at school, we all helped with the threshing. Children's work was gathering the chaff into sacks from under the threshing drum, and trying to satisfy the voracious appetite of the traction engine with seemingly endless supplies of coal, which we brought from our coalshed in a wheelbarrow, and water transported by trolley in milk churns. The engine would draw the water from the churns through a flexible pipe, making a gurgling sound rather like an elephant drinking through its trunk.

Apart from threshing we helped with a variety of tasks on the farm. We helped to turn the hay during haymaking, and to stook the corn after the binder, during the corn harvest. In the spring we helped plant and hoe cabbages, and to thin the crops of mangolds and swedes grown to feed the cattle in the winter. All through the year we helped father in the blacksmith's shop, spending hours working the hand bellows which kept the fire burning in the hearth and helping to weld metal on the anvil. We all became expert at this operation, learning to draw the white hot metal from the fire just as it began to sparkle, placing it quickly on the anvil so that father could follow with the other piece, to place on top to make the weld with blows from his hammer. Speed was essential for success. If the metal was drawn from the fire too soon, the weld would fail; too late and it would be burned and useless.

Shoeing horses took a great deal of father's time and when horses provided the power on the farms before the arrival of the tractor, he attended to the shoeing of some fifty horses in and around the village. In addition to shoeing horses brought to the blacksmith's shop, he would travel out to the farms to attend to lame horses, and to trim the feet of horses on the few farms where there was no road travelling to be done, and no need for the horses to be shod. In addition to all this he was kept busy repairing farm machinery. He worked very hard and it was often difficult to fit his farming in with the work in the blacksmith's shop, particularly when seasonal work was calling for urgent attention.

We spent most of our days within the confines of the parish. Trips to Derby, five miles away, were infrequent and only made during school holidays with either mother or father; both could not leave the farm together. Unlike most farmers, father only went to Derby on market day when he had some business to attend to. He travelled by horse and trap, and if he happened to be going in the school holidays would take one of us with him in turn. When we arrived in town we used to leave Kit, our faithful mare and

Opposite: The authors father, John William Cox, with Kit.

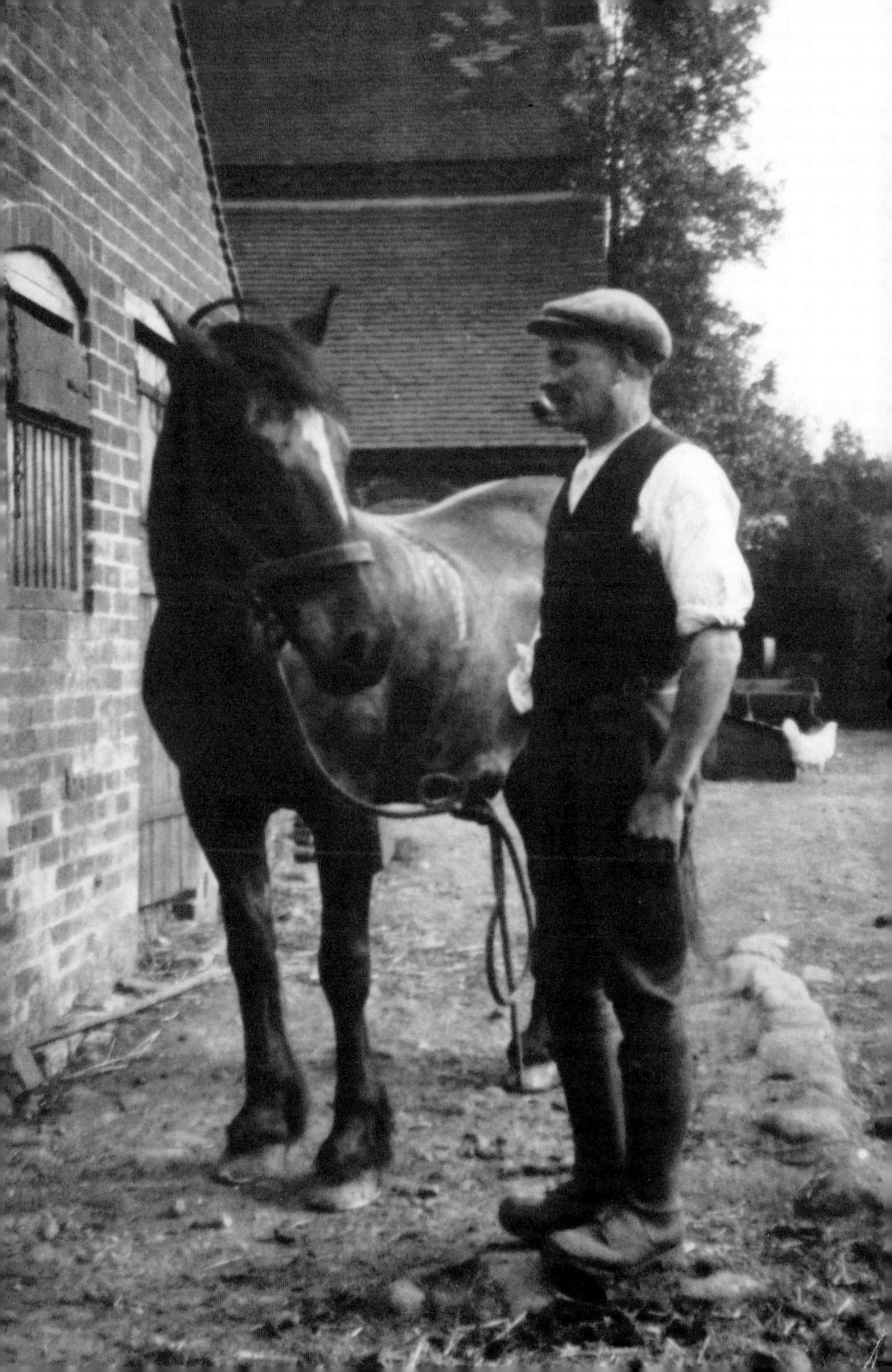

the trap at the Corporation Hotel stables, near the cattle market, and the price charged included rolled oats for Kit, to keep her happy during our stay in town. Sometimes, on the return journey we would call at the gasworks for a supply of small coke called breeze, which was used for the fire on the hearth in the blacksmith's shop at home. On the way home, when we had reached the outskirts of Derby and the town began to give way to the country, father would hand me the reins to let me drive home. He used to say 'just hold the reins loosely'. I always felt very important to be placed in charge, and it was not until years later, thinking back, that I realized that I was not in charge at all. Kit knew the way home without me doing anything about it, and I doubt whether she would have taken any notice if I had tried to divert her from the homeward path. I am sure there is a moral in this somewhere.

Life at Twyford was simple, and in modern terms, as far as material possessions are concerned, we were certainly deprived. It was hard work for the womenfolk, running the homes and bringing up families. There were no modern appliances. None of the houses had electricity (this did not arrive until 1939), no piped water or sewer, and no one had a bathroom. Water was pumped by hand pumps from wells. Lighting was by paraffin lamps and candles, cooking was on a coal fired cast iron cooking range which had to be black leaded once a week. Television was of course years away. Radio had just arrived and I remember we had to keep very quiet at six o'clock each night, while father listened through a pair of headphones to the news and weather forecast, from a temperamental crystal set.

Although we children were happy enough, life was not easy for our parents. Everyone in the village was connected with farming and the twenties and thirties were the years of agricultural depression. Mother and father both worked very hard to make both ends meet, something about which we were largely unaware at the time. Mother always had to make do and mend, and when times were especially difficult father sometimes had to sell a cow to pay the rent for the farm. We never had any pocket money. Our parents could not afford to give us any, and as there was no shop in the village and we rarely travelled, we had no use for it anyway. There were compensations however. What we did not know and had never had we did not miss. Everyone knew everyone and we were related to several families including the Hudsons who were our nearest neighbours — more about the Hudsons later. We were concerned with each others' affairs, and always ready to help one another without interfering. As children we all played together — there was no class distinction. Whether your parents were farmers or only worked on a farm made no difference as far as the church, the school or our parents were concerned. I am sure it is because of this that I have never been conscious of belonging to any particular class.

Apart from life at home, we paid frequent visits to our Uncle's farm at Stenson, a mile away. We, who had never travelled far, regarded Uncle William as a bit special, because he had been to London, and had seen the crown jewels! We spent much of our holidays there, and often helped with the harvest. There was much to interest us at Stenson. The farm was crossed by two railways and the Trent & Mersey canal, and we would often sit by the canalside to watch the narrow boats which we called barges. Nearly all were horse drawn. It was unusual to see one engine powered. All were owned by Fellows, Morton & Clayton, possibly the largest boat owners in the country. The prows of the boats were painted in bright colours and adorned with jugs and buckets, gaily painted with roses and other flowers. One railway through the farm was the LMS Derby to Birmingham line where it was joined by a branch lane. Trains often had a long time to wait on the branch line, and to while away the time, the engine crew would throw lumps of coal at rabbits in the field. The rabbits came to no harm, but the men's efforts left quite a lot of coal lying in the field, so there was no need to purchase any. All engines were steam driven, and the railway company was responsible for fire damage to crops caused by sparks from the engines. At harvest time the corn was cut by binder, before the advent of the combine harvester, and we used to help to gather the sheaves of corn into tent like groups called stooks, where they were left to dry out before being carried to the farmyard by wagon. For 22 yards, alongside the railway line, however, we left this to the railway men. They would set up the sheaves in extra long stooks at that distance from the line, to limit the company's liability in case of fire.

The main line had a level crossing, a signal box and a crossing keeper's house, where the Raynor family lived. Uncle had land on both sides of the line, and was entitled to use the crossing. Mrs. Raynor was the crossing keeper, and when the crossing was needed, would open the gates, having previously checked with the signal box that the line was clear. Mr. Raynor worked on the railway, and we used to play with the Raynor children.

Sometimes we would climb the steps into the signal box and felt very important to be allowed, with help from the signalman, to pull the heavy levers operating the signals. The signal box was bright with geraniums and other flowers, and the ground about was cultivated by the railwaymen as allotments, with more flowers, and orderly rows of vegetables. All was neat and tidy. It is very different now. The house and signal box are gone, and all is derelict and overgrown. Only a solitary lilac bush in what was the garden blooms each spring as a reminder of how it used to be.

A lane leading from Twyford to the village of Findern is known as Frizam's Lane was supposed to be haunted. Nervous people would not travel alone there at night. This was supposed to be on account of a certain Gypsy Frizam who committed suicide and was buried there with a stake of holly through his heart! There were stories of pigs being seen crossing the lane, and horses and dogs taking fright. One night, my father, a level headed person, and not at all superstitious, saw what he thought was a pig crossing through the hedge on one side, and out through the other. He was sufficiently concerned to visit the following morning, and to note that where the pig had crossed the hedge was so thick on both sides that an animal could not possibly have penetrated. I had never seen anything out of the ordinary myself, and had almost forgotten these stories until, on reading Sir George Crewe's diary, I noted that when he was riding along this lane in 1832, his horse 'Cupid', 'jumped at what I cannot tell — bolted down the lane, started afresh at some water passing through a small bridge — bolted through an open gate — quite frantic, with his head up; he bid defiance to all my powers to stop him'. Eventually, Sir George was able to stop Cupid and dismount and after calming him down by 'patting him and using kind words', was able to return to Ticknall, leading his horse most of the way, crossing the river at Twyford Ferry.

When we reached eleven years of age we had to leave Twyford School, and I went on to the Bemrose secondary school in Derby. I left the village school at Twyford with only happy memories of my early years there. Although I may have acquired more knowledge later on, I believe I learned more of real value at Twyford than anywhere else. When pupils left Twyford School they were not only literate and numerate, but all knew the difference between right and wrong, which was not, as so often now, a matter of opinion or the subject of debate, and the Church and our parents taught the same standards. That is not to say that former pupils never departed from these standards, but they were always there in the background, to remind and call us back. Regrettably the same cannot be said today.

My years at secondary school were uneventful. In my final year, which coincided with the outbreak of the second world war, I managed to matriculate but had no thought of going to university. I did not have a scholarship and my parents could not have afforded the fees. At first I wanted to become a teacher, but the outbreak of war interfered with many plans. For some time I had little idea of what I wanted to do, and I know this caused my parents some concern. I was interested in so many things but could not decide on anything in particular. This inevitably led to a certain amount of drifting, and 1941 found me at a government training centre in Leicester which was geared to the war effort and there I trained as an engineering draughtsman. This was followed by four years at Rolls Royce in Derby which found me in a career which I would not have chosen, but in the circumstances could not avoid. I did, however, have plenty of time to think things over and decide what I really wanted to do when circumstances permitted. I did not want to follow in my father's footsteps but wanted to something connected with the land and with the countryside. I was inclined to become bored with doing one thing for any length of time, and was looking for something with variety. In the end it was reading Constance Holme's book 'The Lonely Plough', a novel based on a landed estate in Westmorland, that helped me to make up my mind, and I decided I wanted to become a land agent.

That settled, the next problem was how to begin. There was no family background to the profession, but after talking the matter over with my father, who seemed relieved that I had at last made up my mind what I wanted to do, it appeared there might be a solution close at hand. The Calke Abbey Estate, of which our farm formed a part, was managed by an agent Mr. A. J. Hooley from an office at Ticknall. Unlike my father, I had never met Mr. Hooley on his infrequent visits to our farm, but on father's suggestion, I wrote to him, telling him of my ambition. In reply he asked me to call on him and one Saturday afternoon shortly afterwards, I cycled over to see him. He lived at a house called The Priory, a large house on the edge of the village, where the estate office was situated in a converted coach house in the yard. Mr. Hooley could not have been more helpful. He took me into the office to show me round and we had a very pleasant discussion. He gave me advice about how to proceed, suggested subjects for study and before I left invited me, when I was free, to accompany him on some of his duties around the estate, so that he could show me more of what was involved in the profession. This was far more than I could possibly have hoped for, and during the next eighteen months or so, I used to cycle over to Ticknall on Saturday afternoons and during holidays. Before long I was helping him to take levels for drainage schemes and to survey properties for repairs. His help was most freely given and I soon began to learn a lot about an interesting and varied profession. This arrangement suited me very well, and it was certainly a great help to me. However, as time went on, I felt I wanted to become more involved and accordingly, one day, I asked him about the possibility of becoming a pupil in the office.

With all the work he appeared to have to do single handed he needed someone to help. I was a little disappointed when he told me that there might be a possibility one day, but in the meantime he would prefer things to carry on as they were, advising me to continue with my studies and my present work. I had no alternative but to accept this, but felt that one problem was that he did not want his routine disturbed by taking me on a full time basis. A few months later I mentioned the matter again. This time he was more encouraging but said that before anything could be arranged I would have to be interviewed by Mrs. Mosley.

I was of course, happy to agree to this and asked if he would make the necessary arrangements. Never one to move rapidly, some time passed before he told me that he had arranged for me to present myself at Calke Abbey one Friday evening at seven o'clock. It was November and at that time I had never seen Calke Abbey; in fact I had never been in the park, and since by this time I had visited most parts of the estate that goes to show what a private place Calke Abbey and the park were in those days.

I thought I had seen Calke in 1938. In that year I was still at school and with other subjects studied church architecture. One Saturday afternoon we were taken by our master to study the churches at Melbourne and Repton. We travelled by cycle and on the journey from Melbourne to Repton, the road ran alongside the Calke Park wall. (This was in the days before the Staunton Harold reservoir had been constructed.) Dismounting and looking over the wall, I saw what I thought was Calke Abbey — a building with a glass dome surrounded by a high brick wall. On returning home, father looked puzzled when I announced that I had seen Calke Abbey. After questioning me, he explained that what I had seen was not Calke Abbey, but the Orangery in the gardens; He told me Calke Abbey was hidden in the valley below and could not be seen from the road.

Father had been to Calke however, and told me how to get there. I remember him telling me to enter the park at the Ticknall Lodge, follow the drive along the lime tree avenue through Ticknall Park, past the Middle Lodge where Agg Pegg the keeper lived, then on through the park proper, past Betty's Pond, afterwards turning left to follow the drive down to the Abbey itself. This sounded straightforward enough. I knew it would be dark at that time in November, but what neither my father nor I reckoned on was a foggy night as well, it was in fact, the worst night that winter, as I cycled over from Derby after work. From Ticknall village I did not have too much difficulty in following the drive to the turn beyond Betty's Pond, but from there my troubles began. I thought I would begin to see the lights of the Abbey, but fog prevented this. I did not know then that even without the fog no light would have been visible from the shuttered windows. Cycling on I came eventually to a large gate which I opened and leaned my cycle against a brick wall surmounted by wooden railings. From there I walked a few paces until a huge building loomed up out of the gloom. I assumed this to be the Abbey, but a closer inspection revealed that it was built of brick so I knew this must be the stable block. Before this the fog had caused me to become somewhat disorientated, but finding the stables gave me back a sense of direction. I crossed over again to where I had left my cycle, and followed the wall until I came to a wooden gate. With some trepidation, I opened the gate and followed a path down through trees until I came to an area paved with flagstones. Walking across these flagstones, suddenly I saw through the gloom, the massive bulk of the Abbey itself. Everywhere was in darkness, not a chink of light to be seen anywhere.

I felt my way, groping along the stone work of the house until I came to a massive oak door which I thought must be the front entrance. I searched for a bell but all I could find was a massive wrought iron latch. I knocked several times, each time louder than before but no one came. I was beginning to despair and decided I must try elsewhere. Moving along a few yards I came to a corner in the building, then further on another. After groping my way round three of these, I came to the front entrance under the huge portico, and after more fumbling in the dark, found a brass door bell. I pulled on this several times but could hear no sound of ringing. I was now getting quite desperate, and began to pull the knob in an agitated manner. This worked and I heard the bell ringing. I discovered afterwards that the bell wire was slack, and this was the only way to make it work. Once I heard the bell I waited, and after what seemed an age, the door began to open slowly and an elderly lady in a black dress with white cap and apron appeared, holding a candle. She seemed surprised to see me, and it was obvious that she was not expecting anyone to call, certainly not at that hour.

I told her who I was, and my reason for calling, whereupon she asked me to go in and invited me to sit on a high backed chair just through the door, saying she would tell Mrs. Mosley of my arrival. She then left the hall taking the candle with her and leaving me in total darkness. After some minutes, a door opened on the other side of the hall and Mrs. Mosley came in also carrying a candle, and sat on a chair as far from me as possible. With the light of one candle in that large room, I could hardly see her, and I am sure she could not see me. When she began to talk to me it was obvious that she was almost as surprised as her maid to see me. It appeared that Mr. Hooley had spoken to her about me and it had been agreed that I should call on her sometime but nothing had been definitely arranged, and she was certainly not expecting me that night. However that did not seem to matter. She said she was only sorry that I had had to make the journey on such a bad night.

During our conversation, little was said about the work in the estate office, which was understandable, because Mrs. Mosley could not be expected to have any detailed knowledge of its working, but she was aware that Mr. Hooley was in need of assistance, as he was working single handed since his clerk Miss Atkins, had left to join the forces, and had not yet returned. We did however, talk about the estate in general and I mentioned my family's connection with it going back over one hundred years. In particular I mentioned my great aunt Hannah's association with the Purchas family of Alstonfield on the Harpur Crewe's North Staffordshire Estate. The Reverend W. H. Purchas had been vicar there for many years, and previously had been at Calke in the 1850s as chaplain, and tutor to the young Vauncey Crewe, Mrs. Mosley's father.

This strange interview lasted about ten minutes and as we talked, the mounted heads of the long horned cattle looked down on us in the flickering candlelight, no doubt wondering what it was all about. When it was over, Mrs. Mosley thanked me for calling, said she would speak to Mr. Hooley and hoped I would have a safe journey home. When I left Calke, I found the fog had lifted slightly, and I found the return journey much easier. I arrived home with a feeling of relief that the interview was over, I hoped I had made a favourable impression and the final obstacle had been removed. However when I saw Mr. Hooley again I found he had still one more card to play. He told me that Mrs. Mosley was favourably impressed but he was not yet in a position to engage me. He went on to explain that he would want me to work, not at the estate office at the Priory but at the Estate Yard in the centre of the village where he planned to open a sub-office. This was the headquarters of the estate maintenance staff. Mr. Marriott, the estate foreman lived in a cottage there, and was in charge of the yard which consisted of a sawmill, joiner's shop and builder's yard, all of which had been converted many years before from former farm buildings. I knew that Mr. Hooley and the foreman never got on well, and he told me that he wanted to have complete control of the estate yard, but could do nothing while Mr. Marriott was there. He was nearing retirement, but there was no question of asking him to do so. That sort of thing never happened at Calke. After listening to all this I was in deep despair, thinking that I would never achieve my ambition.

Shortly after this however, differences between agent and foreman came to a head. I shall never know what really happened but there was apparently an altercation between them one day in the estate yard, which led to Mr. Marriott resigning on the spot. That was exactly what Mr. Hooley wanted and he immediately took control of the estate yard and the maintenance staff. He then converted a room attached to the foreman's cottage to form an office, and, true to his word, sent for me to offer me the post I had waited patiently for so long. All this coincided with the return to civilian life from the Observer Corps of Miss Irene Atkins to take up her old post of secretary, having joined Mr. Hooley's firm on leaving school.

Arthur John Hooley was the fourth of the professional land agents who served the Harpur Crewes for over a hundred years. The first professional agent, Thomas Grime was appointed by Sir George Crewe in 1841. He was followed by John Shaw in 1872 who in 1849 had founded the firm which later came to be known as Shaw and Fuller, and until 1940 the family estates were managed from the firm's offices in Derby.

John Shaw who was agent to both Sir John and Sir Vauncey, was born in 1826. Trained as a surveyor, he was engaged in a number of railway surveys in the 1840s and was also involved in enclosure and other Parliamentary work. As land agent to the Harpur Crewes and other wealthy clients, he was an important person in his own right. He lived in style in his own property, Normanton House, an imposing 18th century, residence in what was then the small village of Normanton by Derby, long since engulfed by the outspread of the city, although Normanton House still stands today, being part of Homelands School. John Shaw was important in his profession, and in 1900 was elected President of the Surveyors Institution, the forerunner of the Royal Institution of Chartered Surveyors. As agent to Sir John, he was much involved in the improvements being carried out on the estates, including the building of new farmsteads and cottages. At home at Normanton, John Shaw took a leading part in the religious and social life of the village. He was a churchwarden and first Chairman of the Parish Council when these were formed in 1894. Living at Normanton House, the most important house in the parish, he was regarded as squire of the village. We are told the family dined on oysters, and Mrs. Shaw expected the women who lived in the village to curtsy then they met her in the street. One of John Shaw's sons, also called John, joined his father in the firm. A striking figure, well over six feet tall, he spent some time managing the Harpur Crewe North Staffordshire Estates, where he lived at Alstonfield Manor. Not noted for his industry however, his main interest in life was sporting, and he formed a pack of beagles to hunt in the district.

Thomas Alfred Fuller was born at Aston Tyrrold in Berkshire. He came to Derby to join the firm and in due course became a partner. When John Shaw retired, he became agent to the Harpur Crewes. A tall spare figure, dignified and reserved, he was a competent surveyor who undertook his duties in a quiet professional manner. When he visited the tenants he always appeared to be in a hurry to get away – perhaps because he was afraid of being overwhelmed by endless requests for work to be done. He saw

John Shaw. *Thomas Alfred Fuller.*

the Calke Abbey Estate through the difficult years of the first war, and into the agricultural depression which followed. He lived at Littleover, the neighbouring village to Normanton where John Shaw had lived. Throughout his career he upheld the Harpur Crewe tradition. He died suddenly in 1926 and the inscription on his gravestone in Littleover churchyard reads 'His ways were ways of pleasantness and all his paths were peace'.

When Mr. Fuller died he was succeeded as agent by Mr. Hooley. Mr. Hooley who was born in 1871 was a native of Derby who joined John Shaw's firm as a pupil on leaving school. A polite, unassuming person of great patience, always polite and courteous, he has been described as one of nature's gentlemen. He took over the management of the estate at a difficult time during the agricultural depression with falling rent rolls, and within two years of the death of Sir Vauncey with the burden of death duties and the general state of disrepair into which the properties had fallen during the Sir Vauncey era, when the emphasis had been on game preservation to the neglect of farming. This combination of circumstances meant that Mrs. Mosley and her agent inherited problems which they were never able to solve completely.

Mr. Hooley, like his predecessors, managed the estate from the firm's offices in Derby. For many years he lived at Rose Cottage, in Allestree, a village north of Derby which over the years had become a suburb of the town. Here he was much involved in local affairs, being a churchwarden, parish councillor and President of the village cricket club. He was also a member of the old Belper Board of Guardians, and later served on the Belper Rural District Council of which he became Chairman.

Opposite: Arthur John Hooley.

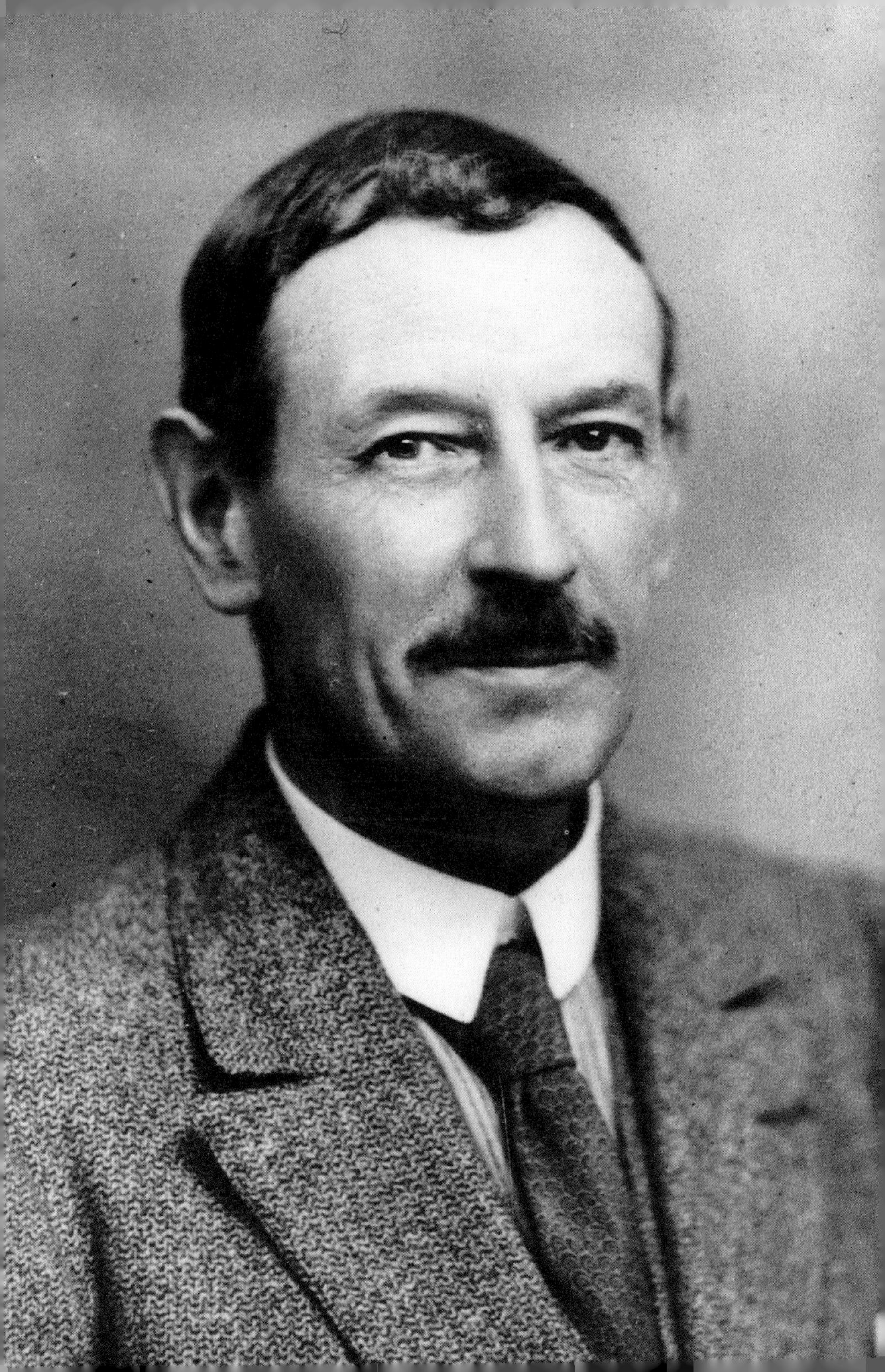

With the outbreak of war in 1939, Mrs. Mosley felt that with the additional problems this would bring, she would like her agent to be nearer to her at Calke. In 1940, The Priory, a pleasant Georgian house on the outskirts of Ticknall, became vacant and she asked Mr. Hooley if he would move there. At first he was reluctant to do so. The move would mean leaving Allestree where he had lived among his friends for many years, and closing his office in Derby. Eventually he agreed but I do not think the Hooleys were ever really happy at Ticknall. Mrs. Mosley owned practically the whole of the village and Mr. Hooley, as her agent, was much involved in the management of the properties as part of his professional duties, but the family still regarded Allestree as their home, and paid frequent visits to keep in touch with their friends.

    To prepare for the move to Ticknall, the coachhouse at The Priory was converted to form an estate office. In the event, Mr. Hooley moved in before the work was completed; in fact it was never finished. This was mainly due to the fact that most of the estate staff involved in the work left to join the forces. As a result, concrete floors were laid but never tiled, some of the walls were left unplastered, door frames fixed but the doors themselves were missing. An upper floor reached by means of a loft ladder had been constructed, but the floor boards which had been sawn in the estate saw mill from green poplar timber were laid loose, and had warped badly so that nowhere was the floor level. This floor was used for storage and it was here that boxes of papers and piles of plans, which had been transferred from the Derby office could be found. The fact that the work had never been finished never seemed to worry Mr. Hooley; in fact he often used it as a ready made excuse when tenants called to complain about work which had been started but left unfinished. He would show them round the offices and point out that he, the agent, had been similarly treated!

    This was the situation when I started my career as Mr. Hooley's pupil in the estate office at Ticknall.

Chapter Two
My life on the Estate

IF, when I started work, I had entertained any notion of introducing changes in the office, I would have been sadly disillusioned. Fortunately, by this time I knew Mr. Hooley well enough, so no such thought entered my head. He was a law unto himself. He had operated alone for so many years and had no intention of allowing anyone, least of all a pupil, to disturb him in his settled ways. Those who today are trained in modern office techniques would have been appalled by the lack of any recognisable system. The office did not possess a single filing cabinet, only a number of deed boxes and chests of drawers in which files were kept. On his large partnership desk was a permanent jumble of papers, but he always seemed to be able to extract from this pile whatever was required, and put his hand on a particular paper immediately. He did not install a telephone at the estate yard office and the one at the Priory office was of the old fashioned variety, with the mouthpiece on a stand and a separate earpiece. There was an extension to the house, and when a private call for Mrs. Hooley was received, a handle had to be cranked to ring a bell in the house. The telephone was operated manually from the exchange at nearby Melbourne by Miss Hastings. This was a great help because when Mr. Hooley was leaving the office on estate business, all he had to do was to tell Miss Hastings, and she would inform incoming callers that he was out, and the time of his return. In this way, she was really part of the office staff, and when the exchange became automatic and she retired, this service was no longer available. To mark her retirement, and to show our appreciation for the help she had given us over the years, Miss Hastings was presented with a bouquet of flowers.

During the four years Miss Atkins and I were at the estate yard office, I would call at the Priory office each morning to discuss the business of the day with Mr. Hooley, and bring instructions back for both of us. and he would make notes on any scrap of paper which was to hand. I remember my first day at the office, when he took from the pile of papers on his desk what looked to me like a final demand for tax, turned it over and proceeded to write a note on it for me. I felt bold enough to draw his attention to what appeared to me to be the importance of the piece of paper. When I did so he replied 'I know perfectly well what it is, but I only pay taxes when it suits me, not when it suits the Collector of Taxes'. This was part of his philosophy. He never allowed anyone to tell him what to do or when to do it. His polite and gentlemanly manner always seemed to enable him to get away with anything. I never knew him to lose his temper and he was always able to calm down irate tenants who called at the office. On rare occasions a tenant who was not getting his own way with the agent, would threaten to see Mrs. Mosley at Calke Abbey. To this Mr. Hooley would respond by saying quietly: 'Well you know you are quite at liberty to do so if you wish'. That would settle it, and the tenant went away knowing he had lost the argument, and the battle.

When the office was opened at the estate yard there was a minimum of furniture, but no typewriter, There was an old Royal standard model at the Priory office which Miss Atkins had used in the old days in Derby, but Mr. Hooley seemed reluctant to part with it even though his secretary had now returned and needed it to do her work. His explanation was that he might wish occasionally to type a letter himself. It was almost a year before he could be persuaded to release it. Until then if Miss Atkins needed to use the typewriter she had to get off the bus from Derby at The Priory, type the letters and afterwards walk down to the estate yard. After she had gained possession of the typewriter, she would still alight at the Priory to take dictation before walking to the office to type the letters which Mr. Hooley would call in later in the day to sign.

Although letters were typed, envelopes were always addressed by hand; the typewriter must never be used. We were allowed to lick the envelopes before sealing if we wished to do so, but Mr. Hooley never did this. He always moistened the envelope after dipping his finger in a jug of water which he kept for this purpose on a windowsill at the Priory office.

Mr. & Mrs. Hooley always spent two weeks holiday in Skegness because, he told everyone "It does us most good". He did not give up his duties however, even when on holiday, and kept in touch with us, so for these two weeks his office address was "The Waverley Hotel, South Parade", opposite the bowling green, where he spent much of his time.

Soon after my arrival at Ticknall, I became very much involved in the practical work of the management of a large estate, consisting of many farms, smallholdings and cottages, and a large acreage of woodland. The differences between agent and estate foreman having come to an end with the latter's resignation, Mr. Hooley had the complete control which he wanted. He did not appoint another foreman, and virtually placed me in charge of the maintenance staff almost from the beginning. All this was new to me, and it was very much a case of learning by doing, but I soon established a good working relationship with everyone. Mr. Marriott, the retired foreman, continued to live in his cottage in the estate yard. He was always friendly and never interfered with what I was doing. I understood that one or more of the estate staff had hoped to succeed him, but this would probably have led to jealousy and ill-feeling. Mr. Hooley was no doubt aware of this and decided that the introduction of a stranger in their midst would be the best solution. At our daily meetings at the Priory. I would report on the previous day's work, and he would give me general directions and guidance, but I was left largely to my own devices.

It soon became apparent to me that the staff only needed encouragement and a sense of direction, and before long the estate yard became a hive of activity. At that time the staff consisted of two sawyers, three joiners, two bricklayers and their labourers, a blacksmith and a painter and decorator. Working in the woods were three woodmen cutting timber. Some of the timber was hauled to the estate yard for conversion into fencing materials for supply to the tenants, while the best was converted for use in the joiners' shop. Other felled timber was converted in the woods by axe cleaving, to provide fencing material to keep the miles of woodside fencing in order, the repair of which being the responsibility of the estate. The woods were managed on the selective system, i.e. trees were selected for felling scattered over the woodland area, and seedlings were encouraged to grow to take their place. This avoided clear felling, and preserved the general appearance of the woods. There had been some compulsory clear felling during the war but this was discontinued afterwards.

Estate Yard at Ticknall.

During the years when the Royal Show travelled round the country before it became established on its permanent site at Stoneleigh, the Calke Estate always supplied the silver birch used in the jumps for showjumping. Each year towards the end of June, a lorry load of birch branches, tied in bundles, had to be got ready for collection by Edward Wood of Derby, the main contractors for the show.

Billy Dexter was the woodman in charge. He was a real country character, and an all round craftsman, having spent a great deal of his life in the brickyards and lime quarries at Ticknall. He was an accomplished blacksmith, and at one time worked in the blacksmith's shop attached to the quarries. The quarries closed down on the outbreak of war and did not reopen. When I arrived on the scene, Billy was working in the woods, and still did all the blacksmithing required to keep the woodmen's tools in working order. In the woods he would split the larger tree trunks into manageable sizes using gunpowder. The powder he used was left over from limestone blasting in the quarries. He kept it in a secret place known only to himself. I knew better than ask him where he kept it, and I doubt if he would have told me had I done so. I was fascinated to see him in operation. He would bore a hole in the tree trunk with an auger, pour in the powder from his powder flask, place the fuse in position, then pack the charge with brick dust rammed home with a wooden peg. I always retreated to a safe distance before he lit the fuse, to wait for the explosion.

Billy lived in a cottage in Ticknall, close to the brickyard where he used to work. He would have nothing to do with mains water, and always fetched his supply from a spring behind his cottage. He always claimed that tea made with water from the tap was not fit to drink.

Properties on the estate were not in good repair in those early days. There was still evidence of neglect from the time of Sir Vauncey, who was always more interested in sporting and natural history than farming, coupled with the agricultural depression between the wars, followed by further decay during the second war when building controls prevented much being done, and some of the estate maintenance staff were away in the forces. When I arrived several members of the staff had only recently returned.

Following my arrival, a start could be made with emergency repairs to roofs, doors and windows, so that properties could be made watertight, and painting, which had been neglected for years could be put in hand. The properties were taken village by village. The builders would first be set to work on the roofs, and I would then travel out with the joiners to check and measure for repairs to doors and windows. All travel was by cycle. When everything was ready for a particular farm, I would arrange for the tenant to collect the made up joinery and materials for the painter from the estate yard. This he usually did with tractor and trailer and I would take the opportunity to send along materials, for the repair of nearby cottages at the same time.

My days soon became fully occupied. Apart from the occasions when I accompanied Mr. Hooley in his car round the estate, all my travelling was by cycle or on foot where the cycle could not go. There was always the daily journey from my home at Twyford, a round trip of fifteen miles, and in addition cycling round the estate supervising the staff, inspecting properties for repair, collecting cottage rents, making surveys and taking levels for all sorts of purposes. In most cases I was left to my own initiative, but Mr. Hooley would always accompany me for surveys when the work could not be done single handed. Surveying was his speciality and in this he was a perfectionist. He always insisted on survey work being carried out strictly in accordance with the text book, never allowing me to get away with anything less. When taking levels, all the readings had to be carefully entered in the level book and checked and cross checked according to the rules — there must be no short cuts. I wonder what he would have thought of me if, later in life, he had caught me working out some simple levels on the back of an old envelope! No matter what the purpose of the levels, he liked to have these recorded as heights above sea level if at all possible, and this meant tying the work in hand to the nearest sea level reference recorded by the ordnance survey on the maps, and marked by means of what are called 'bench marks' on some permanent feature such as a building or wall, or in some cases a gatepost. To do this we had to take a line of what were called 'flying levels' from the nearest bench mark which might be a quarter of a mile from where we were working. There was however an exception to this rule in Calke Park, for the simple reason that there were no bench marks to be found there. Mr. Hooley explained to me that their absence was due to the fact that when the government surveyors were recording levels during Sir Vauncey's time, although they had a right to enter the park, they hurried through as quickly as possible to avoid an encounter with either the baronet or his keepers with their shotguns! They preferred not to linger long enough to leave bench marks as a permanent reminder of their visit.

Apart from all this outdoors activity, there was endless work for me in the office, keeping records, report writing and preparing plans. I also assisted Miss Atkins with the clerical work, preparing rentals, rent notices, receipts and statements of account for clients, and for tax purposes. The variety of the work appealed to me and I became totally absorbed. For one who had for so long had not been able to make up his mind what to do, I had found the ideal. There was so much happening and so many different things to do, there was never any risk of becoming bored.

All this work, inside and out, kept me busy enough but I had also to consider the important matter of qualifying in my chosen profession. During the time I had been with Mr. Hooley on a part time basis, I had on his advice, done a certain amount of reading of related subjects, but the time had now arrived to put my studies on a more formal basis.

When I discussed this with Mr. Hooley, it was obvious that he wanted me to follow in his footsteps and qualify as a chartered surveyor, as he had done some sixty years before. However perhaps because I had begun to wish I could have gone to university, I decided to read for an external London University B.Sc degree in estate management. I knew this would mean a lot of hard work, but I must confess that at the time I did not realise just how much time and effort would be involved. When I told Mr. Hooley what I had decided, I remember him asking me if I knew what I was taking on. Having made the decision, I first had to apply to the University for entrance. I had obtained matriculation exemption before I left school but had never registered this, so that process had now to be gone through. This accomplished I began the degree studies by correspondence course through the College of Estate Management, supplemented by what local technical college evening tuition I could obtain. This was not easy because of the limited demand in the area for many of the subject I had to study, but I was able to get some help with economics, accounting and valuation at either Derby or Nottingham Technical Colleges.

I well remember receiving the first correspondence course papers on accountancy to be confronted with a statement on the first page, that it was assumed that the student was fully conversant with the system of double-entry bookkeeping. My problem was that I had never even heard of double-entry book-keeping, let alone be fully conversant with it! I turned in despair to Miss Atkins who of course knew all about it. Helpful as always, she came to my rescue and brought all her old night school text and exercise books to the office for me to study. The double entry system mastered with her help, I was then able to move on to further study.

I often stayed late at the office to study in the quiet, after the days work was done. I remember Wednesday evenings in particular. That was practice night for the church bell ringers. They never disturbed me — in fact I found the sound of the bells quite a pleasant accompaniment to my studies. When they had finished practice, the ringers would return home, but I would still be there at my books, often staying until nearly midnight before cycling seven miles home. In addition to this there were the weekly trips to Derby or Nottingham for evening lectures. Each year there were the university examinations, first at Nottingham, which took London University examinations before it obtained its own charter, and later at London University's examination hall at the Imperial Institute in South Kensington, This burning of the midnight oil seemed to go on for ever but the time came when it was over, having reached a successful conclusion. Graduation Day in London when graduates were presented to the Queen Mother as Chancellor of the University was one of the highlights of my career.

I shall always be indebted to Mr. Hooley who enabled me to enter my profession and trained me during my early years at Calke. He always maintained the highest professional standards and would, I know have been greatly concerned about the declining standards of today. After Mrs. Mosley's death in 1949, he remained with her successor for a short time but the old order had changed. He was now approaching eighty years of age and retired in 1951. He was succeeded at Calke by Christopher

Preston and I stayed on as his assistant until 1956 when I succeeded to the firm of Shaw and Fuller which had been founded by John Shaw in 1848. When Mr. Preston left Calke in 1960 I became agent for the estates, a position I held until the end of 1969.

Chapter Three
Some Favourite Tenants

THE Calke Abbey Estate farm rents were collected half yearly at Ladyday (25th March) and Michaelmas (29th September) and there were collection points at various places on the estate, to suit the convenience of tenants. Most cottage rents were collected quarterly, and in my early days, Miss Atkins and I used to be taken round the cottages in the outlying villages by taxi to collect the rents.

There were special arrangements at Ticknall. Here what was called the 'Ticknall Cottage Rent Audit' was held at the Estate Office to which tenants brought their quarterly rents. Practically, the whole village belonged to the estate, and on rent audit days there would be a steady stream of callers throughout the day.

Rents over the whole estate were low and in the case of the cottages, many were no more than nominal payments, the average rent being about three shillings (fifteen pence) per week and in many cases that included rates. Mrs. Mosley was a benevolent landlord by any standard!

At the Ticknall Cottage rent audit, the first person on the doorstep when we opened the estate office was Miss Dunning who lived in the village with her aged mother, who never believed in being in debt for a moment — so much so that she would sometimes waken her daughter at two o'clock in the morning to remind her that it was rent day, and the rent had been due since midnight. She gave her no peace until she left for the office with the rent money.

The rent audit was an opportunity to inform the agent about repairs or to complain generally. Some tenants. no doubt mindful of the low rents, never seemed to trouble the landlord for anything, and often undertook minor repairs themselves, but others, usually those paying the least, would demand all sorts of things. One of these was Mrs. Hannah Archer, who was quite a character, and I used to pull her leg regularly. She would come into the office, place a pound note on the desk for which she had to be given 1/- (5p) change for thirteen weeks rent, including rates. She would then proceed to tell me all that was wrong with her cottage. I used to remind her that alphabetically she was top of the list of tenants, paid the lowest rent, and always had the longest list of complaints. With her usual smile she would reply that the rent she paid was all the cottage was worth and regarding repairs she only asked for what was necessary. She was however a favourite at Calke and always went away with a promise of something, perhaps a new lid for her washing copper, or repairs to the firegrate.

Another of my favourite tenants was Mrs. Warren of White House Farm on the northern boundary of the estate. A lady of ample proportions, she was always sitting in her chair in front of the kitchen fire when I called. In fact I never saw her doing anything else. She liked to tell me the story of how the Crewes came to own the property. She was apparently living there when the farmhouse and buildings were put up for sale by the then owner. The Crewes would have an interest in purchasing because they owned the farmland, but not the homestead. Mrs. Warren recalled that Mr. Fuller who was the agent at that time called to see if the Warren family as tenants were interested in purchasing. obviously wishing to find out if his clients had a rival bidder. Mrs. Warren told me she answered him by saying "We are certainly not interested. Who in their right mind would want to buy a tumbledown property like this?" She went on to tell him that she did not even intend to go to the auction sale, and that whoever bought it was welcome to it. However, on the day of the sale she decided she would go, just out of curiosity. Accordingly she put on her coat and hat and walked over the fields to the public house at nearby Shelton Lock, where the auction was to be held. She told me that when she entered the auction room, the bidding was in progress and she was just in time to see the property knocked down, but did not know who had bought it. As she was about to leave, Mr. Fuller came over to her and said "Well Mrs. Warren. you will not have to leave White House Farm, I have bought it for the estate." To this Mrs. Warren replied. "You need not have worried about us having to leave, I don't know that we want to stay anyway". However, stay they did, and she was still there all those years later to tell me the story.

White House Farmhouse, although substantially built, was not in a good state of repair. The estate kept it wind and watertight but I was anxious to do more and carry out some improvements including installing a bathroom, but I was never allowed to force these things on unwilling tenants. It was obvious to me that Mrs. Warren did not wish to be disturbed, because whenever I mentioned my plans to her I always got the same reply. "Don't worry your head about this place, young man. It is too far gone to do anything with, and will only tumble down if you start interfering with it. Go upstairs into the far bedroom and you will see daylight coming through everywhere." However, inspite of Mrs. Warren's gloomy predictions, the house stood for many years afterwards.

For many years, Mrs, Annie Ford kept the Post Office with a small farm attached, at Swarkeston, one of the estate villages. When she retired she moved to one of the thatched cottages in Calke village, or Calke Town as it was called in the old days. At Calke, as at Swarkeston. Mrs Ford was a popular person in the community, always ready to help anyone. She was in fact a great organiser of everything and everybody, but did this in such a way that no one ever took offence. When she called at the Estate office to pay her cottage rent, she would take over, during the time it took to write out her rent receipt! A keen gardener with an old fashioned cottage garden with flower borders edged with box, one of her hobbies was growing tulips from seed saved from her own flowers and she produced some interesting colour variations.

Mrs. Ford had a wonderful Christian faith with complete trust in God. One day she told me quite cheerfully that she felt she was coming to the end of her days and said "I have asked the Lord to take me when he can," apparently not wishing to inconvenience Him in any way. She went on to say "I do not mind much when it happens, but I would prefer not to collapse in the road on a bitterly cold day".

Next door to Mrs. Ford, lived Mrs. Hallifield. Their bedrooms were next to each other and in case either was taken ill during the night, Mrs. Ford had devised a system on communication by means of taps on the bedroom wall with a walking stick which each kept by her bed, the number of taps indicating the nature of the illness. She was a staunch supporter of the conservative party, which she always referred to as the conservatories. Eventually, Mrs Ford was called up yonder, and during her funeral service in Ticknall Church, Miss Hudson, her neighbour, whispered to me 'Doesn't it seem strange not to have Mrs. Ford in charge?' I expect however, she had planned everything with the vicar beforehand.

Mr. & Mrs. Matthew Wain lived in a cottage at Stanton-by-Bridge, another estate village. Both active church workers, Mrs. Wain was popular as the organiser of coach outings for the villagers. Her husband had worked on farms in the district all his life, and in an active retirement was the sexton and looked after the churchyard. To him death was a natural part of life, and the gateway to Heaven and he counted it a privilege to dig the graves of parishioners, many of whom were friends who had, as he put it, "gone on before". His faith was such that when in doubt about what to do in any situation he would pray to God for guidance. He said to me on one occasion when he had been in some difficulty; "I have asked Him and he has told me what to do". It was a privilege to know people like these, and from them one learned more about a living faith than from any number of theologians.

Mr. & Mrs. Matthew Wain.

Some cottage rents were collected weekly and this was one of my duties in the early days. Every Monday, I used to cycle over to Smisby, a small village on the southern boundary of the estate, and I remember some of the tenants there particularly well. One was Miss Bailey who lived in a cottage in Forties Lane. To enter her cottage was to take a step back into Victorian times, and she always dressed to match, in a long black dress with a large brimmed hat held in place by a silk scarf tied under her chin. She was an interesting person whose memory went back a long time, and she would often talk to me about village life in the old days. I remember one day enquiring about the cottage drains, because one of my duties was to see that these were kept in order, and was somewhat surprised when she told me the cottage did not have any. She explained that there used to be a drain from the kitchen sink. but it was always getting blocked and became such a nuisance that one day she mixed a bucket of cement, poured it in and sealed it off, putting an end to the problem. She told me that since then she had always used a bowl in the sink which, she emptied over the garden, where it was good for the plants and the soapy water kept the greenfly off the roses.

Another tenant, Mrs. Walker, lived in School Row in the village, a row of cottages end on to the village street. She was getting on in years and, having decided that her time had come, cheerfully took to bed to await the end. In fact she spent quite a few years there, and I usually went upstairs to have a word with her when I called. The stairs were built of brick, one of only two on the whole estate. She used to say to me "I see you have come up brick hill to see me again".

Further along School Row lived Mrs. Bull, a diminutive person, but what she lacked in size she certainly made up for in personality. She was often standing at the end of the row when I arrived in the village, and was sometimes waiting for me to help settle some dispute in a minor skirmish with a neighbour. Once I arrived on General Election day and, asking if she had been to vote got the reply: "Not likely, you won't catch me voting. I never vote for anybody. They are all the same — only interested in themselves. Other people can vote if they want to but nobody is going to blame me for what goes on in Parliament." I once tried to persuade her to let me put a bathroom in the cottage, but she refused, saying that she much preferred her old tin bath in front of the fire where it was warm.

I always got on well with Mrs. Bull and eventually rose greatly in her esteem. Her mother who was over ninety years of age lived in another cottage across the road from her daughter. The cottage next door became vacant and Mrs. Bull asked if she could move into it to be nearer to her mother. It so happened that this would suit the landlords well, because it was planned to improve School Row, and it would be an advantage to have one of the cottages vacant when the work started. Mrs. Bull was overjoyed when I was able to tell her that she could have the cottage. The following week, she attended the party at Calke Abbey, to mark Charles Harpur Crewe's year as High Sheriff, where the tenants were entertained to refreshments in a marquee on the lawn. I was in the marquee talking to Mr. Grimwood-Taylor, one of the Estate Trustees, when Mrs. Bull came across holding her glass high in the air. Probably not used to Champagne, and perhaps a 'little the worse for wear', she said to him. 'I think Mr. Cox is the most wonderful person in all the world'. Mr. Grimwood-Taylor, who knew Mrs. Bull, was highly amused, and said to me: 'My word you are popular. What noble deed have you done to deserve a compliment like that?'

Ebenezer Banton lived in the Ticknall Almshouses. He was a kindly old gentleman with a long white beard, who would tell tales about the old days. As a schoolboy, he used to help William Atkin the Ticknall clockmaker on Saturdays. Parts for the clocks, including chains, came from Birmingham, Ebenezer used to run along the High Street, dragging a chain behind him, to brighten it and clean off any rust. For each chain he received one penny.

Chapter Four
Calke Abbey

UNLIKE 'A city that is set on a hill and cannot be hid', Calke Abbey can be seen from hardly anywhere. Hidden away in a hollow you come across it quite suddenly as there are no distant views of the mansion, not even in the park. This is no doubt because the site was chosen in the 12th century by the Augustinian canons looking for a secluded spot to build their Priory.

During the years following my first visit to Calke on that foggy November night, I came to know the mansion very well — every room, every nook and cranny. This was when Calke really was a secret place, when few in recent years had entered its doors. The great house, with its seemingly endless rooms and corridors, never lost its fascination for me. The majestic silence of the state rooms in their undisturbed order, the windows always tightly shuttered, the remainder in fascinating disarray, the toys in the Schoolroom scattered around as if the children had been spirited away whilst at play. Other rooms piled high with furniture, books and pictures and stuffed animals and birds, together with the assorted paraphanalia of an extraordinary family. In the Saloon, in one of the glass topped display cases filled with historic items found on the estate, was one object which fascinated me. This was a sword left behind by one of the soldiers of Bonnie Prince Charles's army in retreat from Derby in 1745 and found in a farmhouse at Warslow on the Harpur Crewe's North Staffordshire Estate. I used to wonder what story that could tell!

People would ask me: How many rooms are there at Calke? — How many windows? How many rooms? I did not know, sixty, seventy, perhaps a hundred. How many windows? Some said three hundred and sixty five, one for every day of the year. Of course I could have found the answer to these questions simply by counting, but I never did. Perhaps this was because I did not want to detract from Calke's mystery. Some people thought that Calke must be a gloomy sort of place, but I never found it so. Perhaps this was because the canons from the old Priory, who doubtless walked the corridors, kept watch on the house, and a friendly interest in the proceedings. Of all the treasures at Calke, my favourite amongst the family portraits is that of Lady Frances Harpur by Tilly Kettle which hangs over the fireplace in the Saloon. Some years ago, this picture left Calke on loan to the Royal Academy's winter exhibition in London, and it was strange to see the blank space on the wall. This was the only time I remember any of the contents at Calke to be disturbed and I for one was relieved to see Lady Frances return to her rightful place. Another favourite picture of mine is John Ferneley's painting 'The Council of Horses'. This huge canvas, one of the largest in the collection, hangs on the main staircase. This picture of horses holding a council, in the setting of Calke Park, is based on a fable by John Gay, the early eighteenth century poet and author of 'The Beggars Opera'. Of the old Priory of Calke, nothing now remains to be seen above ground, but over the years, during excavations, carved stones and fragments of floor tiles have been found, and are now on display.

If excavation was taking place anywhere near the Abbey, I always took the opportunity to inspect the excavation for clues to the history of the site. Some years ago when Ben Hyde, the estate builder, was rebuilding the sundial on the south front which involved putting in a new foundation, I asked him to keep a look-out for anything unusual. Sure enough he found a fragment of glazed tile which was identified by the British Museum as dating from the time of Calke Priory. On the north side of the Abbey is a walled enclosure known as the Drying Ground, which in the old days was used in connection with the laundry. This was reputed to be the site of the Priory burial ground. It is recorded that during the time of Sir Henry Crewe who died in 1819, two stone coffins were found where some buildings now stand. They were removed and re-interred in the churchyard. One coffin was believed at the time to have contained the remains of Henry Talbot, son of the Earl of Shrewsbury. After the dissolution, in the reign of Henry VIII, a house was built on the site of the Priory, and some arcading to be seen in the courtyard of the Abbey is a fragment of this 17th century house.

John Ferneley's The Council of Horses, *1850 (Principal Stairs).*

Although almost everything at Calke fascinated me, some things were of particular interest. One concerned the mystery of the State Bed. There was the story that somewhere in the house was what had been described as 'the finest state bed in the kingdom', which was supposed to have arrived at Calke in the 18th century, a gift to Lady Caroline Harpur from Queen Caroline, the wife of George II.

The mystery was that no one seemed to know the truth about the bed — where was it, if indeed it had ever existed — or had it disappeared because it was nowhere to be seen? In the course of my wanderings through the house I had never seen anything remotely like what I thought could be a state bed. Perhaps the nearest I got to it was one day when I was walking through some of the rooms with Charles Harpur Crewe, I noticed a four poster bed with somewhat unusual barley twist pillars. There was a bolster and the tattered remains of very ordinary hangings, and, like nearly everywhere else in the house, the bed was piled high with books, pictures and general bric a brac. Out of curiosity, I asked Mr. Harpur Crewe if there was anything special about the bed. 'Oh yes' he replied, quite casually. 'That is the State Bed'. I must confess I was taken aback and said 'Are you sure?' to which he replied 'Well this is supposed to be the State bedroom and that is the State Bed, I suppose. That is all I can tell you'. With this we moved on, but I could not believe I had just set eyes on the finest state bed in the kingdom! The story of how the real state bed came to be discovered walled up in its original packing case, after his death, is now well known, and I was privileged to be one of the first to see it after it had been discovered.

A room that always interested me, was the Caricature Room near the entrance on the ground floor. When I first saw it, this room was like many of the others except that the walls were lined with hessian under the pictures. We were told that under the hessian were other pictures pasted on the walls, which had been covered up on the orders of a Lady Crewe because they were offensive. I remember once when we were doing some work in the room, we tried without success to prise some of the hessian away so that we could see what was underneath. It was not until just before he died that Charles Harpur Crewe decided to have the hessian removed, and I was surprised to find that the 'offensive' pictures were no more than a series of social cartoons from the late eighteenth century by artists such as Gillray

Lady Francis Harpur, with her son Henry who became the 7th (isolated) Baronet.

and Cruikshank. The work of covering the walls with the cartoons had never in fact been completed, and some of the prints were found in a portfolio waiting to be fixed on a vacant space on one wall. I could never understand what it was about the cartoons that Lady Crewe found offensive. Perhaps it was that she only found them boring, and thought that they would have been better kept in an album instead of being fixed to the walls, to be seen every time one entered the room.

Another particular interest concerned Lady Crewe's Boudoir. In 1964 Charles Harpur Crewe served his term as Sheriff for Derbyshire, as his forbears had done in every generation. In July of that year he gave a reception for the estate tenants, and because they were to be invited to see the state rooms, a thorough spring cleaning was necessary. No one could remember the last time a major cleaning had been undertaken. There were covers to be removed from the furniture, carpets cleaned and furniture dusted and polished.

All this was of course quite beyond the capabilities of two part time domestics. I discussed the situation with Charles Harpur Crewe and it was decided to use the estate maintenance staff who were reliable and trustworthy, rather than bring in unknown people from outside, into what was virtually a treasure house. Accordingly, one Monday morning, a small army of workmen, joiners, builders, painters and woodmen descended on the ancient pile. They all worked with a will, and it soon proved to have been the right decision. Most of the men had worked on the estate all their lives. They had a genuine interest in the house and took a real pride in getting the place shipshape for what was in a way their own event. Fortunately we were blessed with two weeks of hot summer weather, and this in itself was a great help. Carpets could be taken out to be beaten on the lawn in front of the house, and the window shutters were opened to let in the sunshine for the first time in many years.

It was at the start of all this cleaning that mention was made of Lady Crewe's Boudoir. I had heard of this room but did not know where it was. It was, however, considered that this room ought to be opened up and cleaned along with the others, and possibly put on show. Ben Hyde told me he knew where the room was and took me to the entrance door behind a heavy curtain in the library. We found the door locked and no one seemed to know the whereabouts of the key. After some searching however, it was eventually found. Accompanied by Ben, I turned the key in the lock and slowly opened the door. The shutters were of course closed, and the room was in complete darkness. Bearing in mind that there was no electric light in those days, we had to open the shutters before we could see anything. When this was done, the daylight came flooding in and the full glory of the room could be seen — the pictures and furniture, cabinets full of fine china, and a superb collection of Ticknall pottery, the famous Ticknall slipware. The walls were covered with a beautiful green flock wallpaper. I was amazed to see the room in such splendid condition. I cannot explain this, for I naturally expected it to be thick with dust and festooned with cobwebs, but there were none to be seen anywhere. The only evidence that the room had been closed for so many years was a pile of twigs in the firegrate, the result of years of jackdaws building in the chimney. Once these had been cleared up, all was in perfect order.

The tenants' party was a great success. It took place over two evenings, the farm tenants being entertained on one evening, the cottage tenants on the other. I was in the entrance hall with Mr. Charles Harpur Crewe and his principal trustee Mr. Richard Grimwood-Taylor to receive the guests on their arrival, who were then invited to visit the state rooms, the men who had helped prepare the rooms acting as stewards.

Afterwards the tenants took refreshment in a huge marquee which had been erected on the lawn. At that time electricity was being installed in the house, but was not available in time for the party. Some lighting from batteries was, however, provided in the marquee, by the electrical contractors.

One Sunday morning, I was at the organ in Twyford Church, when I noticed a stranger in the congregation. Afterwards he came over to introduce himself. It was Kenneth Whitehead, the well known authority on deer and rare breeds of British animals, who had written extensively on the subject, including an article for Country Life on the Portland Sheep at Calke. During the conversation, he explained that he had always wanted to visit Calke Abbey to see the mounted animal heads, particularly the deer. He knew how difficult it was to gain entry to the house, but had made enquiries to find out where I lived, and had come over to see me in the hope that something might be arranged. It so happened that Charles Harpur Crewe was away for the weekend and I was in charge of the house. I had a certain discretion on such occasions and decided that, although if he had been at home, Charles would have asked me to put Mr. Whitehead off, he could rely on me not to take anyone into the house who could not be trusted. Accordingly I arranged with Mr. Whitehead to meet in the park that afternoon. We first looked at the herd of deer which was obligingly very close at hand,

Tenants arriving for their party at Calke.

Charles Harpur-Crewe in the Drawing Room.

The Library.

The Saloon.

and afterwards went into the Abbey. I opened shutters to let in some light and Mr. Whitehead was fascinated by what he saw, pointing out many things about the mounted heads which were of great interest to me. As we were walking through the anteroom off the entrance hall, he paused and looking up at two heads of what I had always thought were black cattle, remarked 'I see you have specimens of the Chartley

Repairs in the Courtyard.

A Restored Rainwater Head.

Restoring the Clocktower on the Stables.

Repairing the Bakewell Weather Vane on the Clocktower.

Regilding the Clockface.

Harpur Crewe Workmen at Calke

43

and Chillingham cattle'. This was a complete surprise to me and I said 'But aren't Chartley and Chillingham cattle white?' 'So they are' he replied, 'and so would yours be if you cleaned them.' I was now becoming really interested and asked him how best to do this, to which he replied 'Oh just give them a shampoo — that should do the trick'. After he had left Calke, I decided that this should be done as soon as possible. The following day I told Ben what I had discovered and what I wanted him to do, and then set off to Melbourne to purchase a shampoo. The girl assistants in the chemist's shop were highly amused when I asked for a shampoo, and told them what I wanted it for. I asked them to recommend something suitable, and after some discussion they advised a beer shampoo, so armed with two of these, I returned to Calke. It was a hot summer's day, and Ben and I decided to use one of the innumerable hip baths in the house. We took it out on to the lawn & filled it with water. Ben then mixed in the shampoo, and we immersed the heads. The water soon turned as black as ink, and after washing and rinsing, the heads were put out on the lawn to dry. In this way they were restored to their original creamy white colour just as Mr. Whitehead had predicted, and were put back in their place on the ante-room wall.

In regard to the state of repair at Calke, before the arrival of the National Trust, the impression has been given that, in recent years, the Harpur Crewes did nothing but allow the property to fall into decay. That is not so. In addition to the major repairs undertaken by Mrs. Mosley, before the war, much remedial work was undertaken in the 1960s, during my time as agent.

The stables were re-roofed, and the clocktower with the Bakewell ironwork restored. The Abbey roof also received attention, the worst parts of the sheet lead being replaced. I formed the opinion at the time that the roof structure itself was suspect, and advised that an inspection should be made by a structural engineer, before further work was

Calke Abbey shrouded in scaffolding during the National Trust's major restoration. In the foreground are descendants of John Shaw, agent at Calke from 1856–1906. left to right; Mary Shaw, his granddaughter, and Patricia Harby, his great granddaughter.

undertaken. Subsequently, the National Trust carried out all the work needed to put the roof in a sound condition.

The old laundry, on the north side of the house, had a pitched roof in a poor state of repair, leaking water into the ground floor of the Abbey. This was removed and replaced with a flat roof, with the rainwater being conducted away, clear of the building.

After 250 years' service, the backs of the rainwater heads and downpipes had worn away, feeding rainwater back into the fabric of the mansion. Some of the heads had to be completely re-made from sheet lead. As far as possible, the original ornaments were carefully removed, and soldered onto the new heads. Some were, however, beyond recovery, and moulds were made so that they could be cast and replaced. If this essential work had not been carried out by the Harpur Crewes, the property may well have deteriorated beyond recovery.

The National Trust has given the stable block a new lease of life and purpose, although, at the time of writing, there is work still to be done. I remember the blacksmith's and joiner's shops working. They are silent now. The brewhouse, which used to supply the household, has not been used for many years, but is intact, and only waits the restorer's hand for beer to be brewed again.

Inside Calke, a constant watch was kept for outbreaks of dryrot, to receive immediate attention. Limited re-decoration of the state rooms, and the family's accommodation, was carried out from time to time. Perhaps the finest of the state rooms in the Saloon, which I should like to have improved by removing some of what I thought of as clutter, particularly the cases of stuffed animals and birds, some of which obscure the oil paintings. Precedence had always been given to stuffed objects over pictures! I would have removed these for display in other rooms, of which, at Calke, there was no shortage. I had, however, never mentioned this to the family, because I know I would not have had permission to proceed. Nothing had to be disturbed at Calke, — not even Nanny Pearce! Miss Pearce, who had been nanny, not only to the Jenney children, but to their mother, a generation before, lived at Calke until she was 95, and was confined to her room towards the end of her life. A roaring log fire was kept in the room on all except the warmest days, and Airmyne waited on her hand and foot. When the chimney needed sweeping, Nanny must not be disturbed. She was merely covered up with a dust sheet with the rest of the furniture, until the operation was over!

Chapter Five
Calke Park

CALKE Park is not an ancient enclosure and does not appear on Speed's map of 1610. Apart from the area to the north of the ponds containing the stag headed oaks, it has been created by successive owners of Calke. By the middle of the eighteenth century, it was still less than 200 acres in extent. In the days of Calke Priory, there would be no park at all, cultivation being carried out almost to its gates. The strips of land cultivated in mediaeval times can still be seen fossilised in the pasture of the parkland to the southwest of the mansion, and one can picture the peasants pausing in their labours when they heard the angelus bell ringing from Calke Priory in the valley below. The landscaped park we see today, is mainly the work of Sir Harry Harpur and his son Henry, the 6th and 7th baronets.

When I arrived at Calke, the park was still a very private place. Apart from the scouts in summer camp, it belonged almost exclusively to the world of nature, where the fallow deer and Portland sheep roamed in complete freedom. The deer had been there for many years and at one time the herd numbered around a thousand. The elaborate deer shelter in the park testifies to their importance and in those days, a sixty acre meadow at Swarkeston was reserved to provide hay to feed them in the winter. At that time there was a herd of red deer, but the stags were destroyed on Sir Vauncey's orders when one of them attacked Lady Crewe's carriage as she was on her way to Ticknall Church. Without the stags, the herd was doomed, but some of the does survived until the 1930s. The red deer which are now back in the park, were re-introduced by Charles Harpur Crewe in recent years, by purchase from the Wootton Lodge herd near

Fallow deer feeding in Calke Park.

Ashbourne. The flock of Portland Sheep has been at Calke since the early 19th century. These sheep are unusual with their sandy brown legs and faces. Both male and female carry horns and the lambs with their brown coats are particularly attractive. Their origin is unknown, but legend tells us that their ancestors swam ashore to the Isle of Portland from a shipwrecked Spanish galleon. What is certain is that they were once common in that area, and Portland mutton was highly prized. However, as agriculture progressed and quantity took precedence over quality, the little Portland sheep could not compete with the larger 'improved breeds' and they declined in popularity. By 1953, the Calke Abbey flock was the only one left in the country and in danger of

Portland sheep in Calke Park.

extinction. However, in 1956 Charles Harpur Crewe gave ten ewes and a ram to a friend in Bedfordshire, and another flock was established. Since then other small flocks have been started elsewhere and the Portlands live on. When the sheep were first brought to Calke, W. Youatt, the author of 'Sheep, their Breeds, Management and diseases', doubted the wisdom of taking the sheep to Derbyshire for, as he observed 'no purposes, however of economic utility can be served by carrying this curious breed beyond the narrow limits where it has acquired the characteristics which are proper to it'. Later on, however, Professor Davis Low, writing in 'Domesticated Animals of the British Isles' claimed that 'they supported well this change of climate and situation'. There is no doubt they are hardy and tend to prefer grazing on the rougher pastures in the park. Their survival at Calke for some 150 years confirms the Harpur Crewes' faith in the breed. In his diary, Sir George Crewe records a visit to the Isle of Portland in 1835, where he purchased a ram and sixty ewes from the foundation flock, to supplement his own at Calke. He attributed the small size of the sheep he had purchased, compared with his own flock, to the very poor quality of the grazing there.

Another feature of Calke Park, alas no longer there, was the heronry in the Serpentine Wood to the north of the ponds. It became established when nesting birds arrived in 1893, and to encourage the birds to stay, Sir Vauncey had trout put in the ponds nearby to make sure there was sufficient food close to hand. The heronry reached its peak in 1927 when 70 nests were recorded. After this it began to decline and the last nesting birds left the site in the 1960s. Although they no longer nest in the park, herons can still be seen fishing, standing like grey statues by the water's edge. Perhaps one day they will return to nest. During the time of Sir John Crewe, the farmer baronet, long horned cattle were part of the scene at Calke, and were exhibited nationwide. Nothing now remains of these noble animals save a collection of mounted heads, and oil paintings of prize animals which can be seen in the house.

Over this wildlife sanctuary which was Calke, Agg Pegg the keeper reigned supreme. Agathos Daniel Pegg was the fourth generation of his family to occupy Middle Lodge as gamekeeper to the family. No one could remember the time when there was not a Pegg there, and the succession to the post of Headkeeper was automatic. As Harpur Crewe succeeded Harpur Crewe at Calke, so Pegg succeeded Pegg at Middle Lodge. Agg Pegg became Sir Vauncey's confidant and friend. He travelled with him on his natural history expeditions both at home and abroad, helping him to amass the vast collection at Calke, much of which can still be seen today.

Agg Pegg, one of the long line of Calke game keepers.

The outbreak of the last war brought some changes to the park. The Ministry of Agriculture decided that, in the interest of food production, the park must be grazed by something more useful than a herd of deer and a few ornamental sheep. Consequently the herd of deer was ordered to be substantially reduced, and replaced by grazing cattle. The Ministry offered to help but Agg, who did not welcome the idea of strangers entering what was, after all, virtually his private domain, elected to reduce the herd himself, which he accomplished in a relatively short space of time. To stock the park with cattle, it was decided to invite the estate tenants to send their young stock to the park for the grazing season from May to October. Payment was based on so much per head of stock. With agriculture expanding, the tenants were glad of this opportunity to obtain extra grazing. Conditions in the park were ideal with plenty of grass and, equally important, plenty of water and an abundance of leafy shade. One of my duties when I arrived at the estate office was to organise this leystock grazing as it was called. Before the season commenced, application forms would be sent out to the tenants and when these had been returned, the number of stock allocated so that the park would be properly grazed without being overstocked. So that the cattle could be identified, each animal was branded on the hoof and horn, usually with the tenant's initials. Agg Pegg was in charge, and would look round the stock every morning. If he found anything amiss he would report to the office, so that the owner could be informed. This system of grazing kept the park in a reasonable state, but was not ideal, because it was difficult to decide how many stock to take in each year. If the summer was dry there might be a tendency to overgraze, while in a wet summer there would not be enough stock to deal with the abundance of grass.

In 1958, however, a new farm manager, Norman Clarke was appointed. Norman was young and enthusiastic. He persuaded Charles Harpur Crewe to purchase cattle to graze in the park, and to expand the sheep with a commercial flock, thus the number of leystock was reduced and eventually discontinued altogether. At about this time, the estate purchased an implement called a 'Jungle buster' for towing behind a tractor. This was like a very heavy rotary mower with chains instead of a nylon cord. It was purchased primarily for clearing the rides in the woods where it could deal with the toughest of undergrowth, but was also used in the park for clearing unwanted bracken, which was encroaching onto the pasture land from the wooded areas. This combination of bracken control, proper grazing and systematic re-seeding under Norman Clarke's management led in a comparatively short time to the park taking on the attractive appearance it has today.

On the north side, the park takes on its wildest nature, with stag headed oaks and beeches amongst the bracken. It is a beautiful place at all times of the year but is perhaps at its most attractive in the autumn when everything turns to gold. When the deer had free range of the whole park, it was to this wildest part that they would retreat during the rutting season, when the bellowing of the stags could be heard through the autumn mists — a most unmusical sound from such graceful creatures. Later on, in early summer, the fawns would be born in secret amongst the bracken.

On the edge of the park, in Ticknall village, are the Lime Yards, an area of abandoned limestone workings. Long since taken over by trees and bushes, they are now a nature reserve, providing a home for an abundance of limestone flora, including several species of our native orchids which flourish on the floor of the abandoned workings. Here was what used to be called the 'dropping wells'. This was where limestone had

The morning after the collapse at the dropping wells. The author, together will the late George Insley of Lime Kiln Farm survey the scene.

been quarried to form a pool of deep dark bluish-black water below and a cave above. Pillars of limestone had been left to support the roof of the cave from which water dripped constantly into the pool below — hence the name. The pool itself always looked dangerous and forbidding and had, in fact, been the scene of at least one drowning tragedy.

In 1952 the Estate engaged an outside firm of valuers to conduct a field by field survey of the farms for a rental revision. One day in July, I was with the survey party, walking over the land of Lime Kiln Farm on the edge of these old workings. As we were walking over the top of the dropping wells, C. C. Preston, the agent at that time, remarked 'Be careful how you tread, it is hollow under here and could collapse at any moment.' We smiled and carried on, not taking the remark at all seriously. Some twenty minutes later, having finished for the day, we were having tea at the agent's house which overlooked the limeyards when we were startled by a loud rumbling, and looking through the window, saw a cloud of dust rising. The roof of the dropping wells had collapsed just as Mr. Preston had jokingly predicted. The last person to have walked across after us was the farm boy driving the herd of cattle home for milking. It was thought that over the years, pieces of rock had fallen from the limestone pillars supporting the roof, until they could no longer support the great weight above. The ground had fallen about forty feet, and we could only guess what might have happened to us if we had been there at the time. At any rate we made the front page of the Derby Evening Telegraph, with a photograph, and a banner headline proclaiming 'Five men miss death by twenty minutes'!

Chapter Six
The Gardens

SOME visitors to Calke have been disappointed to find that there are no gardens surrounding the house, the formal gardens having been swept away in the late eighteenth century in a landscaping scheme. This was however, a distinct advantage in my day when it came to garden maintenance on a tight budget, it being always comparatively easy to keep the grass round the house in a reasonably tidy state.

In my early days at Calke, however, the surroundings of the house were by no means devoid of interest. The way to the walled gardens from the Abbey takes you through what are called the 'Pleasure Grounds' and until recent years this was a most pleasant part. Under the large trees, some of which still remain, were winding paths through banks of rhododendrons and azaleas, always a mass of colour in the spring, interspersed with hollies, acers and flowering shrubs. In the spring also the ground was a carpet of aconites, snowdrops, crocuses, daffodils, primroses, cowslips, bluebells and many other wild flowers such as bird's eye, ragged robin and forget-me-nots. In the autumn these would be followed by the berries of cuckoo pint or wild arum, and the flowers of hardy cyclamen and autumn crocus. Under the shade of the walls were ferns, periwinkle and hostas. Across the drive from the east side of the Abbey, a winding path led through the trees on the far bank, past the pets' cemetery to the grotto. Amongst the trees were the remains of box, and more rhododendrons.

It is unfortunate that in recent years, when it was decided to confine the deer in the park instead of allowing them to roam wild, the Pleasure Grounds were included in the deer enclosure. Here they did untold damage. All the smaller trees, including some which had been planted to extend the pleasure grounds in recent years, had been destroyed by bark stripping, and the rhododendrons and other shrubs practically eaten away. Close grazing by the deer also destroyed the flowering bulbs, and many other plants. Restoration work has been under taken by the National Trust, but it will be some years before this part has been restored to its former glory.

In one corner of the rose garden, Charles Harpur Crewe planted some bulbs of the 'Fynderne Flower', a species of narcissus, which had been given to him by Miss Marian Bunting of Findern, a village not far away. There is an interesting legend attached to these flowers. It is said that a member of the Fynderne family, ancestors of the Harpur Crewes, brought some bulbs from the Holy Land, when returning from a crusade. He planted them in the grounds of his home at Findern. where they flourished, and spread throughout the village, and were a few survive to this day. Unfortunately, those planted at Calke, and others planted afterwards, have not survived, but it hoped to establish them eventually. with the hope that they may be encouraged to grow wild in the pleasure grounds.

The National Trust has removed the roses from the rose garden and replaced these with bedding plants, harking back to an earlier time. It is now called the flower garden. This I regret, but I am pleased to see the auricula theatre brought back into use for its

The 'Fynderne Flower', given to Charles Harpur-Crewe.

intended purpose. It was not until the National Trust arrived, that I learned it was a rare survival from the early nineteenth century.

The walled gardens at Calke, were laid out on traditional lines, with the walls facing to the four points of the compass, to suit fruit trees requiring different aspects. Alongside the north wall facing south, was the main line of glasshouses, with the furnace house below ground on the other side. Beyond the north wall, a belt of trees forming part of the pleasure grounds, acted as a wind-break.

The Orangery, which I once thought was Calke Abbey, has been restored by the National Trust and is now a fine building. I remember it with the original dome intact, and wistaria and japonicas on the front walls. Inside was a mimosa and a Chusan palm, but the orange trees, for which it was built, had long since gone.

In 1960, the Orangery was in disrepair, and towards the end of my time at Calke, I planned to undertake the necessary repairs, which could then have been carried out at reasonable cost. The glass dome did not collapse, as has been reported, but was carefully dismantled and put aside for restoration. The sash windows required only a small amount of repair. Unfortunately, after I left, the work was not proceeded with. The next ten years took their toll, and I was shocked to find it in a state of dereliction, when I saw it again in 1980. Restoration by the National Trust was achieved only at great expense. In front of the Orangery there was, until the 1960s, box edging of what may have been a parterre or knot garden. Box edging was a feature of the gardens at Calke, and could also be found edging the garden plots of the gardens in Calke village and elsewhere.

The walls of this large garden used to be lined with fruit trees, but most have disappeared. In recent years it has been grassed over for ease of maintenance, but before that, the paths crossing it were lined with espalier fruit trees of which only a few remain. These were old, and to me, unknown varieties, and in the gardens elsewhere there were medlar, mulberry and quince trees.

On the rising ground in front of the Abbey is a small reservoir, fed by a spring. I had discussed with the estate plumber the possibility of piping this to construct a fountain on either the east or west sides of the house.

The early nineteenth century was probably the heyday of gardening at Calke and varieties of plants were propagated and named after the family. Most have fallen by the wayside, but the yellow daisylike Doronicum Harpur Crewe is widely cultivated and the double yellow wallflower Cheiranthus Harpur Crewe is back in favour, after a period of decline. This can only be propagated successfully from cuttings, and was cultivated, not at Calke, but at Drayton Beauchamp in Buckinghamshire by the Revd Henry Harpur Crewe, a well known botanist and gardener, who discovered it growing on a garden wall. It was subsequently brought to Calke but I never saw it there, although it could be found growing on cottage garden walls in Ticknall village.

From time to time, Charles Harpur Crewe and I would travel to Gregory's rose gardens near Nottingham to purchase replacements for the rose garden, when the emphasis was always on scent and colour. On one of these visits, we purchased bushes of the striking red floribunda rose 'Sarabande' which were planted round the sundial, in an attempt to relieve the somewhat sombre front of the abbey. The old house thought otherwise however, and arranged for the browsing deer to see them off!

It is not easy to picture the gardens as they were in the old days, but in their fading glory as I first remember them, perhaps I saw the hand of Lady Crewe, the wife of Sir John, who was a keen botanist and gardener, and travelled widely to collect rare and beautiful plants for Calke.

Chapter Seven
Camping in the Park

WHEN one thinks of Calke, in the old days, as the most secret of places, and recalls that some people living on the doorstep had never been through the park gates, it is perhaps surprising to learn that for many years the scouts had a camp site in the park, which was in regular use throughout the summer holidays, at Easter, and very occasionally in the winter for a few hardy souls. Sir Vauncey would never have allowed this but after his death, permission was obtained through the influence of Captain C. J. Bennett of Normanton, near Derby who was a friend of Col. and Mrs. Mosley at Calke Abbey. Captain Bennett was a veteran of the Boer War and a contemporary of Sir Robert Baden-Powell. The Captain or 'C. J.' as he was known to the scouts, recalled sitting fishing from the harbour wall at Poole, in Dorset, in July 1907 when Baden-Powell and twenty one boys went marching by to set up camp on Brownsea Island, which led to the founding of the scout movement. Afterwards, C. J., returning to his native Derbyshire, was involved for a number of years with the Boys' Brigade, which was associated with the scout movement in its early days. Later on, in 1911 he took charge of the 4th Derby Derwent Scout Group, one of the first to be formed in the county and remained in charge until 1958.

In March 1925, the year following Sir Vauncey's death, C. J. was invited with a party of about twenty scouts, by Mrs. Mosley to see the stuffed animals and birds in Sir Vauncey's collection. They cycled over from Derby, were entertained to tea, and following this introduction to Calke, the 4th Derwent was given permission to camp in the park and to take firewood for their annual Guy Fawkes bonfire at Normanton from a nearby wood on the estate. This permission to camp in the park was later extended to other scout troops in the county and scouts used to come from as far afield as Chesterfield.

The site chosen by C. J. was ideal. It was in a clearing in a secluded spot north of the ponds surrounded by stag headed oaks and other ancient trees, and gave the impression of being miles from anywhere. Close by were the remains of a walled enclosure called The Nursery, where forest trees used to be grown from seedlings, and where the last of the seedlings had been abandoned and allowed to grow wild. According to tradition, this enclosure was the site of an old farmstead, presumably dating back to the days before the land was enclosed in the park. On the camp site was a never failing spring of pure water which must have slaked the thirst of generations of scouts. There was an inexhaustible supply of firewood for camp fires and opportunities to practise many of the skills of camping, particularly woodcraft, and there was always swimming and canoeing in the ponds. Near the camp site was a row of Wellingtonia or Giant Sequoia trees with the characteristic deeply fissured spongy bark, and I wonder how many did

Opposite: C. J. Bennett.

C. J. Bennett.

Father Handford in camp, counting the petty cash.

as I always used to do, punch the trunks with my fist as I walked by, just to prove that this could be done without feeling pain! Not far away was the old boathouse, rapidly falling into ruin, and a flight of stone steps led from Mere Pond to the site of Lady Catherine's Bower, were only the foundations of a polygonal summer house lie hidden beneath the undergrowth. Here, in the eighteenth century we are told, was 'a sylvan retreat where men idled while a musician played'! The scouts must often have puzzled over initials carved deep into the bark of a long dead beech tree nearby, which the revellers had left behind as evidence of their presence all those years ago.

Over the years, the camp site became very popular. Often on Friday evenings in the summer, when I was cycling home from work, I would meet a scout troop toiling up the Stanton Hill on the way to camp, pushing a handcart piled high with camping equipment, no doubt pleased to reach the top of the hill, to be able to coast down to Ticknall and Calke Park beyond.

For some years I was in charge of bookings for the camp site. Supplies of bread and milk were delivered to Agg Pegg at Middle Lodge or Peggs' Lodge as we always called it, because no one could remember the time when a Pegg had not lived there. There they were stacked up outside the lodge to wait collection by the scouts. Agg was a great favourite with the boys. He would take them round his aviary behind the lodge to show them his ornamental pheasants and his collection of game birds, kept for showing, and descended from fighting cocks. He would show the boys his collection of pictures of past champions, and made no secret of the fact that he had taken part in the sport of cock fighting, before it had been made illegal — and quite possibly afterwards! He would also show the boys his collection of stuffed animals and birds, and test them in natural history by asking them to identify the various specimens. He told me he was often surprised by the extent of their knowledge.

Some of the scout masters I remember particularly well. Apart from Captain Bennett, who ran his camp with military precision, there was Father Handford, who brought the Barlow Church group from near Chesterfield. He used to bring along a portable chapel which was set up in a tent complete with altar, cross and candles where services were held. I remember Agg, a tough character if ever there was one, telling me that once when Father Handford invited him to have supper with the scouts, a service was in progress when he arrived, and the sight of the candles and the hymn singing by the boys reduced him to tears!

John Hall-Booth used to bring the 20th Derby St. Augustine's troop. They came complete with band, and would march from camp to Ticknall Church for parade service, with drums beating and bugles blaring. At night this troop would often play a game they called 'Black Spot'. To do this, some of the boys would leave camp after supper and pitch a tent somewhere in the park, to spend the night. From dark until midnight the scout masters would search for them. If found they would creep up and mark the tent with a black spot. The following morning the boys in the tent would look out for the black spot to see if they had been discovered.

On one particular occasion, the scouts were very helpful to me when it was decided to dredge Betty's Pond. This pond, being the top of the chain of ponds or lakes through the valley in the park, is the first to receive water from the stream flowing through Pokers Leys Wood on the park boundary, and as such acts as a natural silt trap. Over the years it had become choked with silt and overgrown with weeds, so that only a

Scouts camping at Calke Park.

sluggish trickle of water was flowing through. Before dredging could begin, it was necessary to drain the pond, and this meant locating and removing an oak plug which we understood was at the bottom of the pond near the dam at the lower end. The estate men had spent some time trying to locate it without success, so I decided to enlist the help of Father Handford's scouts who were in camp at the time. They were only too willing to lend a hand, and the weather was ideal. They brought along their canoe, donned their bathing trunks and first of all hacked through the jungle of weedgrowth to release the sluggish flow. Then with the aid of a long metal rod with a hook on the end which I provided, they quickly located and extracted the elusive plug to release the water. Only then was I able to bring in contractors with a drag line excavator. As the machine worked its laborious way along one side of the pond, the excavated material was spread over the sloping ground as black sludge, completely covering the bracken and grass. It took the rest of the year for the bank to recover its former appearance. Agg came to watch the scouts and the machine at work, and I remember he told me that the pond had been last cleaned out when he was a boy some eighty years before. He explained that in those days the work was done by hand by an army of workmen with wheel barrows and shovel, wheeling the mud up planks to spread on the same bank above.

As far as the scouts were concerned, Calke Park was the finest camp site anywhere and the same troops came year after year. The boys were always so well behaved and never abused the privilege of camping in this secluded spot which no one else was allowed to visit.

Betty's Pond.

Chapter Eight

The Hudsons and Calke

AT the beginning of this story, I mentioned the Hudsons of Twyford who were related to the Coxes, my grandfather, Herbert Cox having married Sarah Annie Hudson in 1889. The Hudson's family connections with the Calke Abbey Estate date back to the 1830s. The family claims descent from Henry Hudson the 17th century navigator, whose attempts to find a north west passage from Europe to Asia are well known, and who gave his name to Hudson Bay and Hudson Strait in north east Canada, and the Hudson river, at the mouth of which New York stands.

The family's connection with the Calke Abbey Estate began with John Hudson, a small farmer living at Breedon-on-the-Hill in Leicestershire with his wife Mary. In 1795 their eldest son John (my great great grandfather) was born, and baptised there on Christmas Day in the Priory Church of St. Mary and St. Harduph, high on Breedon Hill. This John became a gamekeeper at Garendon Park, near Shepshed in Leicestershire and in 1816 married Martha Mounteney from the neighbouring village of Belton. Later on he became a gamekeeper to Sir George Crewe at Calke, and moved there with their five children. This was the beginning of an association between three generations of the Hudsons as gamekeepers, to three generations of the Harpur Crewes spanning nearly 100 years.

In 1840 tragedy struck the Hudson family. In January, one of the sons, William, with his friend John Atkin, the son of the Ticknall clockmaker, both 15 years of age, were returning home from work for breakfast across Calke Park, but never arrived. It was at first thought that for some unknown reason, the boys might have run away from home. When however after nine days of search and enquiry they could not be found, Sir George Crewe, fearing the worst, ordered his men to break the ice and drag one of the ponds near Calke Abbey, when their bodies were found. The boys had apparently gone sliding on the Little Dog Kennel Pond, which is now part of the Staunton Harold Reservoir. It was into this pond that the Abbey drains ran and here, where the ice was thin, it had given way and the boys were drowned. They were buried side by side in a corner of Ticknall churchyard where the grave can still be seen with the text 'Boast not thyself of tomorrow for thou knowest not what a day may bring forth'. The tragedy must have shocked the neighbourhood and in the Ticknall Church registers, the double burial is recorded in beautiful copper plate writing, as if to set it apart from the other entries on the page.

The story of the tragedy was handed down to succeeding generations of children as a warning of the dangers of sliding on ice and is even today, after nearly 160 years, is still recalled by some of the older Ticknall residents. The story is told in a poem entitled 'The Lost Ones' written some years later by my great aunt Hannah Hudson about whom more will be written later. The story is told with great depth of feeling and powers of expression. The countryside in and around Calke Park has changed little over the years, and through the poem it is not difficult to picture the scene of the tragedy, the search for the missing boys, and the anguish of their parents.

Sir George died in 1844, and in 1846 my great great grandparents were still at Ticknall, but later returned to Shepshed. Their eldest son John, (my great grandfather) who was born at Shepshed in 1819, followed in his father's footsteps and was trained as a gamekeeper on the Garendon Estate. In later years he recalled an interesting story from those days. In 1837 he was helping the woodmen to mow the rides in Garendon Park when a messenger brought news of the death of William IV, and the accession of Queen Victoria. Apparently none of the men had heard the strange name Victoria before, and when they were discussing the news, one of the men referred to her as 'This new Queen Vicmaria or what the devil they call her'!

John and Caroline Hudson.

John Hudson married Caroline Dexter of Diseworth, at Loughborough in 1842, Caroline being in domestic service there at that time. When Sir George Crewe died, John, his son and heir, was living near Loughborough and on succeeding to the title and estates, brought John Hudson with him as gamekeeper, and for some years the family lived in a keeper's cottage at Wicket Nook, an isolated spot near the village of Smisby on the Derbyshire — Leicestershire border. The cottage is now part of the National Trust's property. The family lived there until 1858 where seven of their children were born and baptised in the village church at Smisby. In later years the children would recall their childhood days at Wicket Nook, Caroline recalling her parents' shopping trips to Ashby-de-la-Zouch, when a black retriever dog was left in charge at the cottage

— to keep the children in and intruders out. Hannah, about whom more will be written later, recalled childhood days in a number of poems.

During the years at Wicket Nook, the girls attended Lady Crewe's School at Ticknall, which meant a walk of three miles in all weathers. The school was just outside the Ticknall Lodge gates and had a thatched roof. The building stills exists, but is now a residence and tiles have replaced the thatch. The school was for girls only and John, the only boy in the Hudson family at that time, attended the boys' school in Ticknall village. He was however, given the privilege of going to Lady Crewe's School at mid-day to have lunch with his sisters. In 1858 the family moved from Wicket Nook to another keeper's cottage known as 'The Whimsey', now in ruins on the edge of Calke Park near Middle Lodge. The Whimsey was also close to Lady Crewe's School which the girls continued to attend.

Lady Crewe's Free School, as it was known, was built by Sir George Crewe in 1822 as a school for 40 girls, and was under the control of Lady Crewe. At this time there was little education provided for girls. The pupils were chosen by Lady Crewe herself, mainly the daughters of the many employees on the estate, and it was considered a privilege to be selected. The girls wore a distinctive uniform consisting of a neat dress of brown holland material, with straw hat for summer wear, and with a red cloak and hood in winter. On Ascension Day and certain other holy days the pupils could be seen going in procession, two by two, across the Market Place and along Chapel Lane to Ticknall Church, there to sit in the gallery under the watchful eye of Lady Crewe, sitting in the family pew below. Sometimes there would be a tea party for the girls in the courtyard at Calke Abbey and every year a prize giving, with Lady Crewe sitting in state on the balcony, under the entrance portico, the girls sitting on forms below, from where they would climb the staircase to curtsy to her Ladyship as they received their prizes. After the prize giving the butler would serve the girls with tea and iced buns.

At one tea party, given by Lady Crewe at the school, Mrs. Marriott of Ticknall, who as Rosa Shreeve, was the last pupil to be enrolled, recalled sitting by her mother who was asked by Lady Crewe what she would like to drink, to which she replied 'I would like a sup of ale, milady'. When Lady Crewe asked "And what would you like, little girl?", Rosa replied 'I would like a sup of ale as well, milady. To this Lady Crewe said 'Oh no, I think toast-water would be more suitable for you" — and toast-water it had to be. For the uninitiated, toast-water is made by floating a piece of well-done toast on a jug of hot water! — a well known drink in those days, especially for children.

In the classroom, the girls were taught by Mrs. Elizabeth Fox, who lived with her husband in a cottage next to the school. The pupils received a good general education having regard to the times, and Mrs. Fox's capabilities. They were well grounded in the three Rs and in needlework. As a test piece, in needlework, the children made samplers, many of which still exist. Hannah Hudson worked a sampler showing the school and the lodge gates nearby, and later on, another in the form of a family register giving the names and dates of birth of her mother and father, and their thirteen children.

Lady Crewe made regular visits to the school to check on the children's progress, and Hannah Hudson recalled an amusing incident from one of these visits. One morning Lady Crewe came in and said 'Good morning Mrs. Fox, I hope the children are learning their lessons'. To this Mrs. Fox replied 'Oh yes, milady. It is geography this morning and I have just been telling them that Dublin is the capital of Scotland'.

Even Hannah knew better than this, and could hardly wait to rush home at lunchtime to tell her mother what Mrs. Fox had said, although I like to think this mistake was only a slip of the tongue.

Lady Crewe's Free School.

On leaving school, most of the children were destined for domestic service, and the education they received at Lady Crewe's School had this in mind. Before they left, a situation was found, and an outfit, which had been made at the School, was provided. The pupils undertook needlework for Calke Abbey, and when the Hudson children were there they always made Sir John's shirts and socks. Elizabeth Hudson recalled being kept in after school one day, because she was having difficulty in turning the heel of a sock she was knitting. Mr. Fox, who was working in the garden, looked in through the open window when he heard her crying, and when she told him of her plight, he fetched the key and released her from prison. She was not sure what to do with the offending sock, and on Mr. Fox's advice, dropped it behind the large wooden box in which the needlework was kept. I do not know the end of this story. However, about a hundred years later, when I was at the estate office, and it was decided to turn the schoolroom into a residence, I was in charge of clearing the room before the builders moved in. The only items still there from the old schooldays were a sampler, and the old workbox. I remember looking behind the box, as the workmen pulled it away from the wall to see if the sock which had brought Aunt Elizabeth to tears all those years ago was still there!

Lady Crewe's interest in her pupils did not end with their schooldays. She kept in touch with many of them afterwards, and would correspond with those who had left the district, some having emigrated to Australia, Canada or New Zealand.

The Hudson children were under the strictest discipline both at home and at school,

*The author's great-aunts
Elizabeth, Mary, Caroline & Hannah Hudson, who attended Lady Crewe's Free School.*

Hannah Hudson's needlework sampler of Lady Crewe's School.

were taught to behave properly at all times, and to show the greatest respect for the family at Calke Abbey. One day Hannah was swinging up and down on a branch of a tree in Calke Park, oblivious to everything but her own childish pleasure, when suddenly, out of the corner of one eye, she saw Sir John on horseback, watching her. She panicked at the thought that she had perhaps done something terrible. Had she damaged one of his trees, and if so would her father lose his job and have to leave Calke? She was as quickly reassured however, when she saw that Sir John was smiling as he turned his horse and rode away. These were happy days for the Hudson children — there was always something to see and do. The move from isolated Wicket Nook had brought them nearer to Calke Abbey, that great house around which the life of the estate revolved. Nearby were the lime and brick quarries, and the start of the Ticknall Tramway from which the children had picked coal fallen from the waggons when they lived at Wicket Nook.

It is a peaceful rural scene today, but when the Hudsons arrived in 1858 there was great activity all around. The Ticknall lime quarries had been worked for many years for the high quality lime which was in great demand both for building and agriculture, and this had increased following the construction of the Ticknall Tramway in 1802 by Benjamin Outram, the noted tramway engineer. Limestone from Ticknall was transported to Moira colliery near Ashby-de-la Zouch on horse drawn waggons. Unlike a modern railway, these waggons had plain wheels which fitted into the flanged rails of the railway track. When the waggons had been unloaded, they were filled with coal from the colliery for the return journey to Ticknall, so that there were no empty waggons travelling along the tramway. Near the start of the journey at Ticknall, the tramway travelled for 150 yards through a tunnel under Ticknall Park, and then over a bridge across the village street. A brickyard operated across the road from the limeyards. From early morning the children would see carts lined up along the village street waiting their turn to load with lime or bricks, the drivers regaling themselves in the meantime at 'The Royal Oak' or one of several other ale houses close by. Smoke rose from the lime kilns, hanging low over the village on windless days, and from time to time the sound of explosions could be heard as limestone was blasted from the quarry face.

Going home from school along the limetree avenue, the trees looking quite young, having been planted to mark the birth of Vauncey Crewe in 1846, the children crossed the end of the tunnel and would see the horse drawn trucks emerging, laden with either limestone or coal. Along the drive itself the children would see other horse drawn vehicles taking supplies to Calke Abbey, and coaches and carriages with their liveried attendants, taking the Harpur Crewe family or their guests, to and from the great house. All is silent now, the quarries and the brickyard are closed and the tramway, although its route can still be traced across the countryside, is derelict and overgrown. The tunnel and the horse shoe bridge known as 'The Arch', are however remarkably well preserved. The tramway had in fact been in operation for just over 100 years. It was eventually taken over by the Midland Railway and the last loaded truck travelled along the line in 1905. Up to 1913, however, officials of the railway company ran one empty truck in a yearly 'right of way' journey to preserve the right of passage. This annual trip was not always without incident. Occasionally a length of track would be found missing, in which case a length of line which had already been passed over had to be taken up and brought forward to enable the truck to proceed, the process having to be repeated on the return journey. The line was officially closed in 1915, the rails being taken up for scrap, and the land repurchased by Sir Vauncey Crewe.

In those days, Calke Abbey, its state rooms richly adorned with pictures and fine furniture, was not just a great house but a community in itself. In the house, presided over by housekeeper and butler, was an army of domestic servants, maids of all descriptions, footmen, valets, bootboys and messengers, all in their appropriate uniforms. The stables were filled with carriage and riding horses with their attendant liveried coachmen, grooms and stable boys and there was a blacksmith's shop, joiner's shop, bakehouse, brewhouse and laundry. Another army of gardeners looked after the pleasure grounds, and the walled gardens with glasshouses filled with vines peach trees and exotic fruits and flowers. The Home Farm nearby, known as The Dairy, supplied the house with milk and cream, butter, eggs and cheese. A room at The Dairy still preserves the Hopton Stone topped tables, and until recent years the walls were tiled from floor to ceiling.

In due course, three of the Hudson children entered into service at Calke Abbey. While they were there, a domestic magazine called 'The Dog Washers Gazette' was produced based on news of everyday happenings at Calke, collected by the staff, edited by Sir Vauncey's son Richard, and printed by him on his printing press. It is unfortunate that no copies of this magazine have survived, as these would have provided a fascinating insight into life at Calke in those days.

To assist John Hudson with his growing family, Sir John allowed him to graze a milking cow in the park. The cow was looked after by Caroline and the girls, and became so used to female company that when it was sold, it refused to leave the park until Caroline walked in front of it, wearing her shawl.

After a short time at The Whimsey, the Hudsons moved to The Kennels, another keeper's cottage a short distance away and where two more children were born.

In 1860, Thomas Fisher, the gamekeeper at Twyford, seven miles away at the northern end of the estate, died and Sir John asked my great grandfather to take his place. He agreed, and one day the Hudsons piled their belongings onto transport which Sir John provided, and moved to a small cottage holding with some buildings and a few acres, near Twyford Ferry which was to remain the family home for the next ninety years. The land around was subject to flooding from the river Trent, and because of this, the house came to be known as 'Noah's Ark'.

In moving to Twyford, the Hudsons left the wooded undulating countryside around Ticknall and Calke for the flat open landscape of the Trent valley, with a different kind of gamekeeping. The absence of any appreciable cover discouraged pheasants in favour of partridges, but there were the additional duties of looking after the sporting in the river. As at Calke, the game was strictly preserved, but poaching was rife and the keepers were up against gangs of professional poachers, many of whom were desperate characters who would stop at nothing, In the eyes of the law, poaching was a serious offence, and some country parsons, particularly those who were in the pocket of the local squire, regarded it as worse than drink or adultery, and preached sermons against it. Poachers would put down feed corn dosed with brandy or some other spirit, to catch the birds, and after haymaking the keepers would plant thorn bushes in the open meadows, to prevent poachers using their nets. The battle against the poachers was unending. An Act of 1862 had given keepers power to confiscate poaching nets and guns. Some of the poachers were such dangerous men that it was never wise to tackle them single handed. John Hudson had once been left for dead after one encounter with a poaching gang. Referring to this state of affairs, he could recall an incident one dark night when he was walking home from Calke to Twyford. He was climbing a stile in a lonely spot, when he had the unnerving experience of placing his hand on that of another, one of a gang of poachers hiding in the ditch. John Hudson knew it would have been foolish and dangerous to interfere, and he calmly carried on his way. Some years later he was telling this story, and one man in the company admitted that he was one of the gang. He told my great grandfather that he had been wise not to interfere, as they were in a desperate mood that night, and would have stopped at nothing.

It is difficult now to appreciate the passions which game and game keeping generated in those days, and the Parliamentary time which was taken up in formulating successive Game Laws, in attempts to control the situation. It is not surprising that Sir George Crewe, who usually had more important matters to think about, should have expressed the opinion to his son John, that 'it would be quite as well for England if there were not a head of game in existence'.

John Hudson was not always successful in his battles with the poachers and was once outwitted by a local poacher called 'Crowie Smith'. Crowie was the son of a devoutly religious mother, but a no-good father who taught him the worst of ways, and he grew up to become a notorious poacher. He had earned his nickname through his ability to climb tall trees and throw young crows down from their nests.

One night Crowie and his fellow poachers got a large number of rabbits which they hid under one of the arches of Swarkeston Bridge. They then walked to Derby and Crowie was detailed to hire a horse and trap to collect the rabbits. On his way back to Derby, he noticed policemen around when he got to Chellaston, so he drove back to Swarkeston over the river, and then decided to cross the river again at Twyford Ferry so as to put the police off the scent.

Arriving on the other side of the river opposite Twyford village, he shouted 'Boat', which was the recognised way of calling the boatman on the other side. This was a dangerous thing to do because although Crowie was disguised, he knew that the gamekeeper lived close by. As it happened, on this occasion, the ferrykeeper was away and John Hudson took the ferry boat over himself to bring Crowie and his pony and trap across, and put him on his way to Derby. As he drove away, my great grandfather heard a policeman's whistle on the other side of the river. The policeman asked if he had seen a man with a brown pony and trap and wearing a top hat and mackintosh. It was then that great grandfather realised that he had just ferried Crowie over to safety.

Later in life, after being released from prison after one of his many convictions for poaching, Crowie followed a Salvation Army band to the Gospel Hall in Derby where he was converted. Seeing the error of his ways, he spent the rest of his days as a penitent, preaching against the evils of drink and poaching, the profession to which he had previously devoted most of his life.

Not long after the move to Twyford, the Hudson children contracted typhoid fever due, it was thought, to faulty drains at the cottage, and Samuel aged three years, died. His burial was the first in what was to become the Hudson corner in Twyford churchyard. Later that year, the Prince Consort died at Windsor of the same disease, again due to faulty drains, this time at the castle. Typhoid was no respecter of persons. During the children's illness, Sir John showed his concern by sending his coachman daily to the opposite side of the river at Twyford, from where he could call across for news of the children. In this way, he could be kept informed without the coachman having to make direct contact with the family. Such was the relationship between the family at Calke and the Hudsons that on occasions, Lady Crewe would travel to Twyford to take tea with Caroline Hudson. Caroline always produced her best china on these occasions. Once when the Hudson children had chicken pox, Sir John sent his own children over to have tea with them, so that they would catch the complaint. The Hudsons felt highly honoured that of all the other families on the estate who had the disease at that time, they had been selected to perform this service.

In the Hudson household, religious observance was strict, in keeping with the times, with attendance at Twyford Church each Sunday morning and Chapel at nearby Stenson in the afternoon. Caroline Hudson ruled her family with a rod of iron. My great grandmother's strictness in all matters is supposed to have been due in part, to a reaction against the more relaxed style of her own mother, Martha Dexter, who indulged, we were told, in such outrageous pastimes as dancing and playing cards!

Caroline never announced her plans to the family beforehand and if, for instance she decided to go with the pony and trap on the regular Friday market trip to Derby, she would make this known by appearing at the door in her travelling dress. If the trap was already fully laden, enough produce would have to be removed to make room for her.

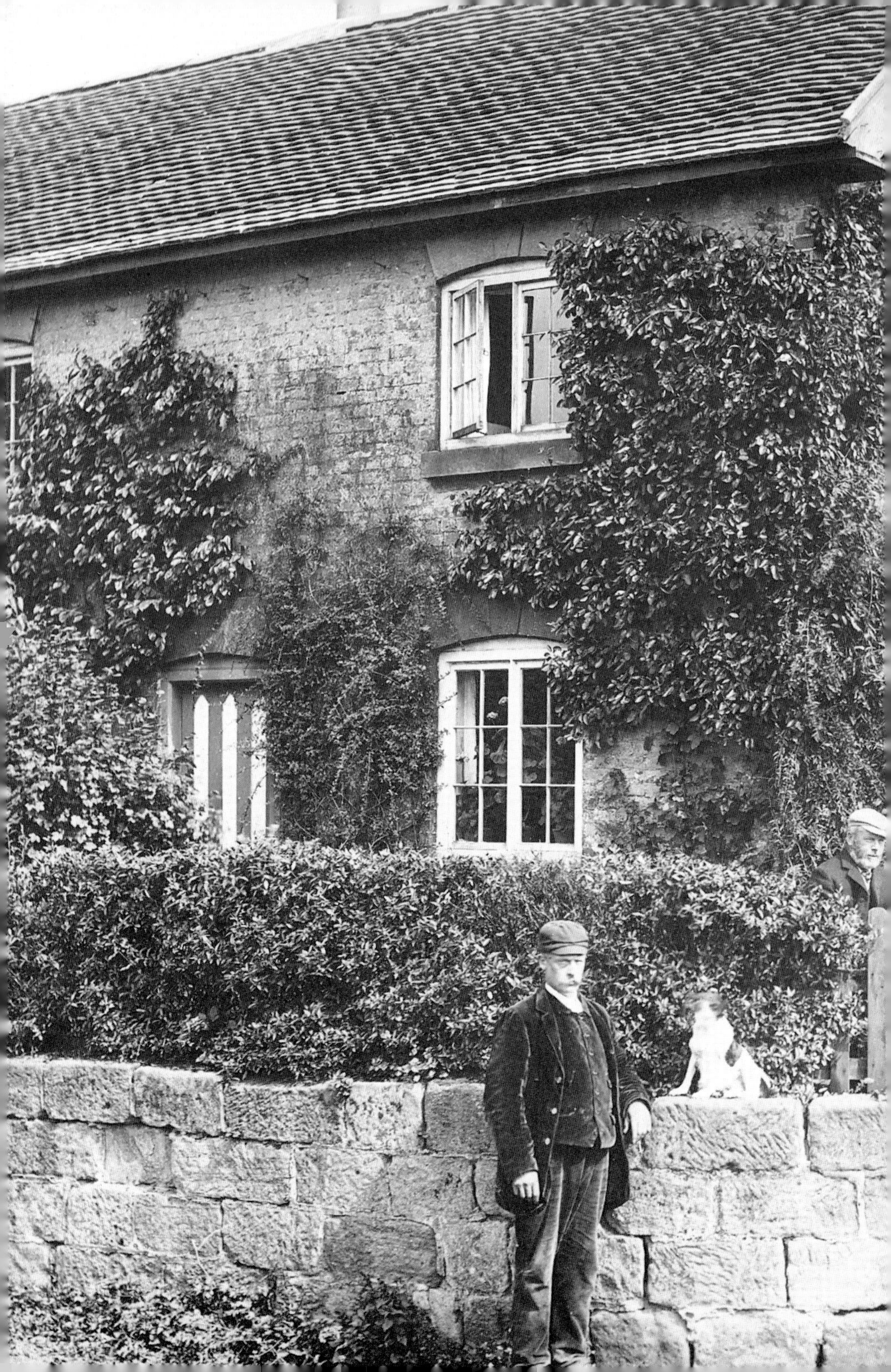

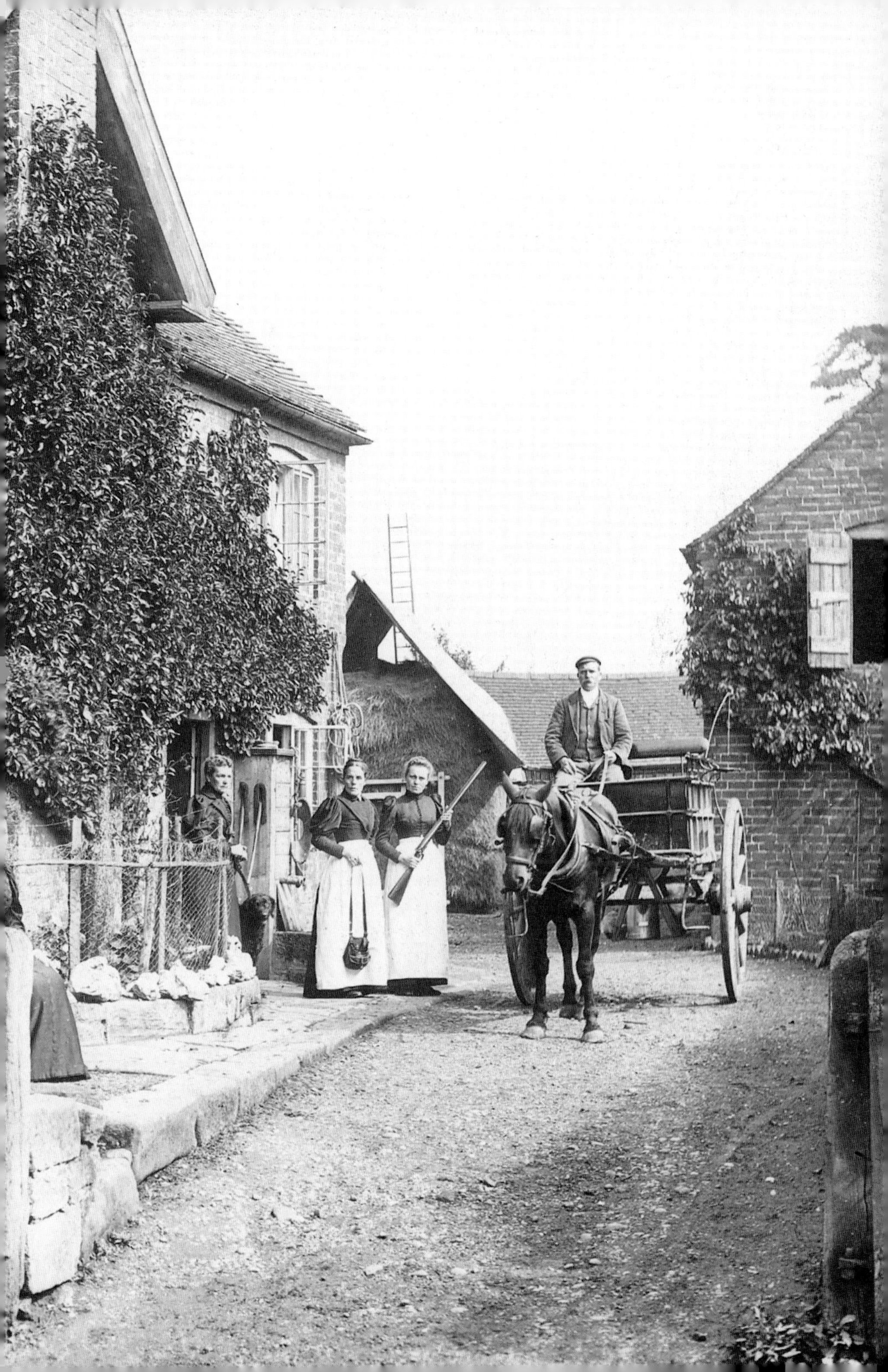

On one occasion, after the children had gone to bed, she noticed that one of the home made cheeses had been nibbled by one of the children, and recognising from the teethmarks that Charlie was the culprit, she went straight upstairs and set about the unfortunate boy with a stick.

Caroline's oppressive regime was such that it was said to be a crime even to laugh in the Hudson household. Not unnaturally this drove the boys at least, to seek entertainment elsewhere, even if this meant no more than going next door to play cards with their neighbour, old Mrs. Jane Gilbert. On these occasions, Jane would hastily spread a tablecloth over the cards, if their mother's footsteps were heard coming along the garden path.

By way of contrast, John Hudson was a kindly man, highly respected by everyone, even the poachers, and was fond of children, having thirteen of his own. If he was inclined to be over-indulgent with his family, it was only to counteract the harsh treatment meted out to them by his wife. Once when she was scolding them he said 'Caroline, I sometimes think that you are a bit too strict with the children,' to which she replied: 'With all this brood, John, if one of us had not been strict, there would have been no room for you and me on the hearth'. On another occasion, when their eldest daughter Caroline, was over from Tissington with her schoolmaster husband, Richard Wain, with their two sons, Richard asked John for pencils and paper, saying that he wished to compare the scholastic abilities of the younger Hudson children with his own. John refused, saying that the children were on holiday and had enough of that at school.

At Twyford the last four of the Hudson children were born, including my grandmother Sarah Annie, who was born in 1864.

In spite of having a large family, or perhaps because of it, John and Caroline had no hesitation in offering a home to cousins, children of the Rice family of Smisby when in 1863, their mother died following a fall from a tree while gathering damsons.

The marriage of Herbert Cox and Sarah Annie Hudson came about as the of what might be called a washday romance. Apparently the Coxes who lived at the blacksmith's shop nearby, had a mangle, something which the Hudsons did not possess. On washday, Sarah Annie used to take the Hudsons' washing over to the Smithy Farm to be put through the mangle, and this led to the couple beginning to show a more than usual interest in each other. When Caroline Hudson heard about this, she decided to buy a mangle to make the weekly visits unnecessary, and hopefully put an end to the romance. This was, however, of no avail and the couple married in 1889 uniting both families.

In 1870, Caroline's mother, Martha Dexter, died and her father William, came to live with the family at Twyford, where he was to remain for the rest of his life. Born in 1800 and over six feet tall, William Dexter had been a shepherd, and brought with him to Twyford a specially made long couch, on which he used to rest at night during the lambing season.

He was quite a character, very stubborn and paid deference to no one. He must have been at times difficult to live with. He was always up first each morning, and if his grandsons did not rise at his first call, would go upstairs, and set about them with a stick. On one occasion when the river was in flood, and water came into the cottage,

Previous pages: The Hudson family outside the Keeper's cottage at Twyford.

driving the family from the kitchen to other rooms at a higher level, William refused to leave his seat in front of the kitchen fire. He insisted on his grandsons setting up his chair on bricks above the water level, where he remained until the water had subsided.

Inspite of this, however, he must have been a useful addition to the family, helping with the cows and chickens, and cultivating the vegetable garden.

Another of William's daughters, Martha, and a son, William, went to work near Waltham Gross some 13 miles from London and their father used to visit them from Twyford, walking there and back — a mere 120 miles each way. He would set off with his belongings tied up in a handkerchief at the end of a stick over his shoulder. The journey took four or five days, with occasional lifts on waggons and carts as he went along. He died in 1883 aged 83 years and was buried at Twyford. The text on his gravestone, was chosen by his grand daughter Hannah Hudson, who was able to quote the appropriate text for every occasion. 'Thou shalt come to thy grave in a full age, like as a shock of corn cometh in in his season'.

John Hudson died in 1894 and was succeeded by his son Arthur, who had been trained by, and had worked with his father since leaving school. Arthur looked after the estate land north of the river for Sir Vauncey, in partnership with his colleague Harry Clarke, a member of an old local family. When Arthur and Harry walked to Derby on Saturday for their weekly night out, the local poachers were on the look out for them, before starting their own activities. When the two keepers became aware of this, they took to travelling separately, and by different routes, so that the poachers could never be sure when the coast was clear. Arthur, who liked a drink, sometimes travelled by pony and trap and when on occasions he got a 'little the worse for wear', Charlie the faithful pony, could be relied on to bring him safely home. Charlie was something of a character. He used to be put out to graze on Twyford Green, an unfenced part in the centre of the village. When he grew tired of this, he would return home, and when he was heard trotting past the cottage, had to be taken back. Eventually he learned to outwit them by walking slowly past the cottage on the grass verge, so that he could not be heard.

Arthur Hudson died in 1916. At his funeral, Sweep, his faithful black retriever, followed behind the procession from the cottage to the Church and sat outside during the service. Following afterwards to the graveside, he took one last look at his master's coffin before trotting quietly home. Thus came to an end an association between three generations of the Hudson gamekeepers, and the last three baronets of Calke.

William Dexter, the author's great, great grandfather

Chapter Nine
Hannah Hudson

AT this point in the story, I must say more about Hannah, perhaps the most remarkable of the thirteen children of my great grandparents, John and Caroline Hudson. I have referred to her birth at Wicket Nook near Smisby in 1848, to her early days there and later at Ticknall. At Lady Crewe's school she received her only formal education, but this was supplemented by a considerable amount of reading which was encouraged by her parents. She made a special study of the Bible, and was able to quote the appropriate text for every occasion. It was during the time the Hudsons were at Calke that contact was made with the Purchas family with whom Hannah was to spend so much of her life.

The Reverend William Henry Purchas was born at Ross-on-Wye, Herefordshire, in 1823. Educated at Durham, his early training was in medicine, but after his father's early death he gave this up and took Holy Orders. In his early years he developed an interest in botany, eventually gaining a national reputation.

In 1857 he was appointed chaplain at Calke, and the following year, became tutor to the young Vauncey Crewe. He encouraged and helped to develop his pupil's interest in natural history, something which was to become the future Sir Vauncey's lifelong passion. Mr Purchas no doubt had a hand in the book *The Natural History of Calke and Warslow* which Vauncey wrote in 1858 at the age of twelve.

After leaving Calke, the Rev. William Purchas served in Gloucestershire until 1870 when he was presented by Sir John Crewe to the living of Alstonfield, an upland parish on the Harpur Crewe's North Staffordshire Estate where he was to remain until his death in 1903. As vicar of Alstonfield he was landlord of a considerable acreage of glebe. The other main landowner was Sir John, who was away at Calke for most of the year and in his absence, Mr. Purchas acted as unofficial squire. He always entertained his glebe tenants to a dinner at Michaelmas.

At Alstonfield, in addition to ministering to the spiritual needs of his flock, Mr. Purchas's medical knowledge became of real practical help to the villagers. It is said that his medical training became apparent soon after his arrival. One day he was called in by one of the parishioners whose husband had been given a bottle of medicine by the doctor. Not only had the patient failed to respond, but appeared to be getting worse. The vicar checked the bottle, and was convinced that a wrong prescription had been given, and advised that no more should be taken until the doctor called again. On his next visit, the doctor, realising his mistake, changed the medicine and the patient recovered.

On another occasion, Mr. Purchas was credited with saving the sight of Mrs. Sutton of Yew Tree Farm in the village. One bitterly cold winter day, her sister came to stay, and was so cold when she arrived that Mrs. Sutton decided that she should go straight to bed with a hot water bottle. She heated the stoneware bottle in the oven but forgot

Hannah Hudson.

to loosen the stopper, with the result that when she took the bottle from the oven, it exploded, scalding her face and temporarily blinding her. The vicar was sent for in haste. He applied poultices to her eyes and attended daily until all was well.

Incidents such as these led to the vicar being called in on other occasions, and always in an emergency which would otherwise have meant a journey of two miles to fetch the doctor, sometimes almost impossible when Alsonfield was cut off from the outside world in winter snow. In fact the vicar's medical services became in such demand that he opened an informal surgery at the Vicarage on Saturday mornings, where advice and simple remedies for his parishioners minor ailments were freely dispensed.

While on his duties about this country parish, Mr. Purchas was able to pursue his interest in botany, and would sometimes take his like minded friends on botanical expeditions. He made a special study of the wild rose, the bramble and the hawkweed and wrote several papers for the botanical societies. He was co-author of *The Flora of Herefordshire*, his native county, which was published in 1889. At Alstonfield he planted oxlips in the vicarage garden and hawkweed in the churchyard, where they remain to this day.

Over the years, Mr. Purchas combined the duties of parish priest with those of squire, doctor and botanist to a remarkable degree. With sincerity, kindness and compassion, he won the hearts of his people and became their never-failing guide and friend.

Hannah Hudson joined the family at Alstonfield as a nursery maid in charge of the young family. She recalled that when she arrived and was introduced to the children in the nursery, the eldest boy Griffiths Thomas, later to be known as 'Mr. Griff', was playing with a box of bricks which had been presented to him by his godmother, Lady Crewe.

At Alstonfield, Hannah entered fully into the life of the family at the vicarage, and the village, and over the years provided valuable assistance to the vicar, both in the household and in the parish, particularly after the death of Mrs. Purchas in 1889. From Hannah's religious upbringing had developed a deep personal faith with complete trust in God's purpose for herself and for all mankind. She had, however, no illusions about the practical problems which life presented, and always had her feet firmly on the ground.

In those days, at Alstonfield, as elsewhere, times were hard and some of the villagers eked out a bare existence with nothing to spare, a situation quite unknown today. If anyone fell sick, a call from the vicar would be followed by a visit from Hannah with beef tea or a custard for the invalid.

Close contact was kept with Calke Abbey and members of the Harpur Crewe family would regularly visit Alstonfield and and other parts of their Staffordshire Estate. John Shaw Jnr. lived at Alstonfield Manor acting as deputy for his father, the agent for all the Harpur Crewe properties.

Each autumn, the whole family would move from Calke Abbey to their north Staffordshire residence, Warslow Hall, for the grouse shooting season. On one occasion, Lady Crewe was over from Calke presiding at the vicarage over a committee of ladies, deciding on the distribution of blankets for the winter to elderly ladies of Alstonfield living alone. The committee was on the point of removing from the list, one lady who had apparently had an illegitimate child in her youth. The ever compassionate Lady Crewe was not happy about this, and turned to Hannah for advice. 'Well milady' said Hannah 'I would say that no matter what she did when she was young, she will

Reverend W. H. Purchas.

need keeping warm this winter.' 'Quite right, Hannah,' replied Lady Crewe, 'she shall have the blankets,' and the committee was overruled.

On one rare occasion when Sir Vauncey was persuaded to open a garden fete at Alstonfield, Hannah bought a pound of tomatoes from one of the stalls and gave them to him. He thanked her profusely. 'You see' said Hannah, 'Everybody thinks that Sir Vauncey has got everything, so nobody bothers to give him anything.'

Hannah had a great sense of humour and was always ready to tell stories against herself. She used to tell the story of the day, soon after her arrival at Alstonfield, when she went by carrier's cart on her first visit to Buxton. When the time came to return she found she was late, and was not sure of the way to a public house called the Cheshire Cheese from where the carrier's cart was due to leave for the return journey. As she was hurrying along the street, she stopped to ask a man the way to the Cheshire Cheese. Mistaking Hannah, of all people, for a lady of ill repute, he began to lecture her about stopping men in the street. Hannah had no time to explain, and taking a religious tract from the supply she kept in her handbag, she thrust it into his hand as she hurried on her way.

On Sundays, Hannah led the singing in Alstonfield Church in her deep and distinctive, slow and measured voice, and the vicar took care that the congregation kept to her pace, particularly during the singing of the canticles. During the summer months, in the country districts, Irish labourers would arrive, complete with sickles to help with the harvest. At Alstonfield, as Roman Catholics, they could not attend the village church and their own church at Ashbourne was too far away. Each Sunday, Hannah, with the approval of Mr. Purchas would hold a simple service for the men on the village green, or in a barn if the weather was wet. The men would sing hymns, and Hannah would lead them in prayer and give a short address. Over the years, these summer services became very popular, and the labourers would travel from the surrounding villages to attend.

It was at Alstonfield that Hannah developed her talent as a writer of verse. She had two distinct styles and a number of her compositions remain. Of particular interest is her poem 'The Lost Ones', in which she tells the story. which she had heard from her grandmother Martha Hudson, of the tragedy of 1840 when her uncle William Hudson was drowned, with a friend in one of the ponds in Calke Park which has been referred to earlier. Another poem 'Day Dreams' recalls childhood days at Wicket Nook where she was born, and in this poem, writing of her old friend Sam Swann who lived nearby, people and places are placed in a biblical situation. There are other poems about family life at Twyford and about Alstonfield. Mr. Purchas, impressed by Hannah's undoubted talents and her knowledge of the Bible, taught her the rudiments of Latin. Always busy in the vicarage household and about the parish, Hannah once remarked in jocular mood. 'When I get to Heaven I hope I do not meet the vicar for he is sure to find me a job to do'.

On January 15th 1898, Mr. Purchas gave a special tea at the vicarage to celebrate Hannah's fiftieth birthday. He called it her Jubilee, and presented her with a studio photograph of herself.

During 1903, the vicar became increasingly infirm, and his familiar figure in clerical dress with gaiters and shovel hat was seen less and less about the parish. His last message to his flock was read from the pulpit on September 13th. He died in December aged 81 years after a lifetime of devoted service to his people. The sorrowing parishioners filed past his body as it lay in state at the vicarage, the faithful Hannah in attendance. He was buried in the churchyard and on his tombstone is the text from II Corinthians 1V.7 which he had chosen himself. 'But we have this treasure in earthen vessels that the excellency of the power may be of God, not of us.'

Both Mr. Purchas's sons, Griffiths Thomas and Arthur, took Holy Orders and Arthur was curate at Alstonfield when his father died. Afterwards he became curate at St. Luke's, Bedminster, a suburb of Bristol, and Hannah joined him there as housekeeper and to help with the parish duties. Life at Bedminster could not have been more different from Alstonfield. Until about 1850 Bedminster had been little more than a village, but grew rapidly from then until the turn of the century. The Wills tobacco factory was established there, and seamen engaged in the coastal trade lived in the district. Here could be found all the social problems of a rapidly expanding working class district, and Hannah soon found herself involved in evangelical and social work connected with St. Luke's parish. Drunkenness and lawlessness were rife, but Hannah was never afraid of becoming involved in any situation. She regarded the work as a challenge, and soon became a familiar figure in her long black cloak, with her Bible under her arm, out with the soup kitchen bringing salvation to lost souls and soup to the deserving poor of Bedminster. Hannah never married, but when recalling those days, she used to say that she had received a proposal from many a drunken man!

In 1910, Arthur Purchas became rector of Stocking Pelham, a tiny hamlet in Hertfordshire, and Hannah accompanied him to assist as before, but in surroundings very different from Bedminster. She spent the last years of her life at Tissington in Derbyshire. Tissington is only a few miles from Alstonfield, so Hannah was able to renew all her old friendships. She was much in demand in the district, and with a talent for preaching would take the service in the Methodist Chapel, often at short notice. She died in 1916 aged 68 years and was brought to the old home at Twyford for burial. On the day of the funeral, the river Trent had burst its banks, making the road to the Church impassable and Hannah's coffin had to be carried across the fields. Both the Reverend 'Mr. Griff' and the Reverend Arthur Purchas were there to pay their respects to a faithful servant and friend of the family. Thus came to its close the life of one of the more notable pupils of Lady Crewe's School at Ticknall.

Chapter Ten
The Early History of Calke

THE early form of the name is "Calc", from limestone which occurs locally, especially in the Ticknall Lime Yards, where it was quarried for many years, and evidence of small workings can be seen in Calke Park.

At the time of the Norman Conquest, the Manor of Calke was held by Algar, Earl of Mercia, whose property was forfeited, but restored to his daughter Lucy, who married the Norman 3rd Earl of Chester, as her third husband. The Earl had inherited vast estates from his father, including much property on the borders of Derbyshire and Leicestershire. He was drowned crossing the English Channel in 1120, as one of the victims of the loss of the "White Ship" but some years previously had founded an Augustinian Priory in what was then a wild but secluded valley at Calke, where the Abbey now stands.

The inhabitants of the Priory were not monks in the strict sense of the word, but ordained priests known as canons, who lived under the rule of the order, but regularly attended to the spiritual needs of the laity in the neighbourhood. They were distinguished from members of other religious orders by their black habit.

According to the chronicles of Dale Abbey c 1150, Serlo de Grendon gave to the canons of Calke, Deepdale (the site of the future Dale Abbey in Derbyshire) where they established another priory. After a few years, however, the canons neglected their religious duties for the delights of the chase, and they were ordered back to Calke in order to preserve the royal deer.

After the death of the 5th Earl of Chester in 1153, his widow, Countess Matilda, founded Repton Priory and ordered the canons of Calke to move there. After that, Calke continued as a religious community, but as a cell, subservient to Repton, after less than 50 years of independent existence.

Following dissolution, in 1538, several families owned Calke before the arrival of the Harpurs. John Priest or Press had leased the property for 99 years from the Priory in 1537 two years before dissolution. With the threat of dissolution, monastic institutions sometimes did this in an attempt to delay the inevitable. In 1537 the Earl of Warwick acquired the property subject to this lease, but he later sold to John Beaumont. In 1575 both freehold and lease were acquired by Richard Wendsley of Wensley in Derbyshire, who sold to Robert Bainbridge in 1585. Bainbridge was a lawyer who represented Derby In Parliament. He was an extreme protestant, who refused to accept the Elizabethan Church Settlement, and was in fact sent to the Tower of London by an infuriated Queen.

It is likely that Calke appealed to him, because the Bishop had no jurisdiction in the parish where Calke Church was a "Peculiar" and he could worship in the Puritan manner without interference. After Bainbridge's death, his son Robert sold Calke to Henry Harpur in 1622. There was a house on the site of the Priory which had probably been erected by Richard Wendsley, and the remains of this can be seen in the courtyard of the Abbey.

The earliest reference to Calke Church is in 1129, but the building we see today is the result of remodelling by Sir George Crewe in 1827. Sir George found the old building 'dark, damp and out of repair, and possessing neither elegance or comfort'. He wanted to show that outwardly at least, 'the Lord's House was not despised or forgotten'. He must have felt the contrast with his mansion of Calke Abbey. Accordingly he built the tower, and encased the medieval nave in new stonework. The church has no chancel, this having been removed by Richard Wendsley, many years before. In the 1980s, Henry Harpur Crewe arranged a service of carols by candlelight at Christmas, which became a popular event.

Seal of the peculiar of Calke.

Chapter Eleven
Harpurs and Harpur Crewes

Harpur. *Fynderne.* *Harpur Crewe.*

The Harpurs are of ancient lineage, and my family's connection with Calke, dating from the early 1800s, during the time of Sir George Crewe, is of comparatively recent date.

The first member of the Harpur family of which we have knowledge is Richard Le Harpour of Chesterton in Warwickshire during the reign, of Henry I (1100-1135). It is interesting to note that the old Norman French word Harpour means Hornblower, which suggests that a member of the family may have been a musician at the royal court.

By the middle of the 14th century, the Harpurs had become established in Warwickshire and Staffordshire, and Sir John Harpur Knt, was Lord of Rushall, a village, now a suburb of Walsall, where he defended his house, described as a Hall with fortified Manor within a wall and moat, during the Wars of the Roses, with a Lancastrian garrison. Sir John rebuilt the church at Rushall about 1444. He died in 1464. Although the Harpurs have long since gone from Rushall, Harpur Road leads to their restored hall, where their crest, a lion rampant, can still be seen over the gateway entrance.

Richard Harpur, son of Sir John's youngest son Henry, studied law. He rose to prominence in the profession and in 1567 was appointed a Justice of the Court of Common Pleas. At a time when property lawsuits were commonplace, he was in a position to earn a substantial income, and turned the experience he gained to his advantage. Through successful property dealings he was able to build up a considerable land holding, mainly in Staffordshire and Derbyshire. An estate in North

Staffordshire, based on Alston field, was purchased, but considerable property in South Derbyshire, in the Trent valley, was acquired through marriage to Jane, the heiress of the Fyndernes, whose family had lived in the village of Findern, south of Derby, and from which they took their name.

The Fynderne coat of arms featured a chevron between three crosses. The bottom arm of each cross was pointed, unlike the other three, which resembled the arms of a Maltese Cross. It was not unlike the preaching cross carried by early itinerant priests, which could be driven into the ground when required for open-air preaching. It is possible that this choice for the family arms, may have been influenced by an ancestor, John de Fynderne, who became a priest in 1400.

Richard chose to live in a house he had built for himself at Swarkeston, some five miles away, rather than in the old manor house at Findern. Of the old home of the Fyndernes there is now no trace, but there are the remains of the house at Swarkeston, and the nearby Harpur Chapel, attached to Swarkeston Church, contains family monuments including the tomb of Richard Harpur and his wife Jane.

The tomb in Swarkestone Church, of Richard Harpur and his wife, Jane Fynderne, founders of the Harpur fortune.

Sir John Port, Jane Harpur's uncle, who died in 1557, provided in his will for the foundation of a grammar school at Repton, which was later to become the well known public school. He made Richard Harpur, one of his executors and his descendants became closely involved with the management of the school. The head of the Harpur family has ever since been one of the four hereditary governors.

Richard and Jane Harpur left two sons, John and Richard. John inherited most of his father's estate, including Swarkeston. Although he had been trained in law, he did not follow the profession, devoting his time to the management of his extensive properties. He became a Justice of the Peace and much involved in local affairs, becoming one of the most respected persons in the county. He was knighted in 1603 and died in 1622.

Sir John had five daughters and seven sons, but only three sons, Richard, John and Henry survived to adult years. Each was provided with his own estate. Calke had been purchased for Henry in 1622 from Robert Bainbridge, son of the ultra protestant owner.

In 1626 Henry purchased a baronetcy.

John Harpur of Swarkeston's son John, had been provided with an estate at Breadsall, north of Derby, but following a series of untimely deaths in the family. when the Breadsall line failed in 1677, the entire Harpur estates passed to Sir John Harpur of Calke, the 3rd baronet, and grandson of Henry, for whom Calke had been purchased. The Harpurs were now firmly established at Calke as large and wealthy landowners, second only in Derbyshire to the Devonshires at Chatsworth. Sir John died in 1681, leaving his son John, his infant heir to succeed him as 4th baronet. He came of age in 1701, and the following year married Catherine, the youngest daughter and co-heiress of Thomas, the second Lord Crewe of Steane in Northamptonshire.

Soon afterwards, Sir John began building the present mansion, to be known as Calke House, on the site of the old priory, demolishing in the process, most of the Elizabethan house which had succeeded it. Lady Catherine was perhaps the first of the Harpurs of Calke with a social conscience, her main concern being the welfare of the tenants and others less well placed than herself. She died in 1745, three years after her husband, and, as evidence of her humility, directed in her will that her son Henry should spend £150 on a plain monument to his father in Calke Church. "I will have no sort of monument myself" she declared. In the event however Henry paid the sculptor Henry Cheere £200 for the handsome marble memorial to Sir John and Lady Catherine which can be seen in the church. The inscription pays tribute to her even when allowance is made for the somewhat extravagant language of the time.

"She was a lady of so rare a disposition that it is hard to say in which of the duties of life she excelled the most for she was eminent in every one. In the profession of religion she was steady, in the practice of it exemplary. She looked upon her birth and station, not merely as marks of distinction but as spurs to the noblest actions. She thought earthly greatness received its fairest lustre from virtue and piety. Though she was placed far above want herself, yet affluence could never abate her humanity. She had the most merciful feelings for the distress of others and she made the miseries of fellow creatures her own. The poor found in her a sure patroness, the orphan a never failing friend."

Lady Catherine's name lives on in Dame Catherine's School in Ticknall, which she founded.

Sir John and Lady Catherine's son Henry, who had succeeded as 5th baronet, had been educated at Oxford and this was followed by foreign travel including the "Grand Tour", in order to prepare him for his position as head of the family, and possessor of a great estate. In 1734 he married Caroline Manners, daughter of the Duke of Rutland. Unfortunately, after only a short tenure of seven years at Calke, he died in 1748, just before his 40th birthday, to be succeeded by Henry, the elder of his two sons, who was to become known as Harry.

There now follows some account of the last owners of Calke, based on my own and my family's memories.

Chapter Twelve
Sir George Crewe

ARTHUR TOPLISS of Ticknall, a painter and decorator on the estate maintenance staff, was a great admirer of Sir George Crewe. When he was a boy, which would be around the time of the first World War, he used to go into the churchyard to talk to Arthur Kirkman who, although getting on in years, was still mowing the grass and keeping the graves in order. There Arthur Kirkman would entertain his young friend with stories of the old days. Arthur told me that no matter how the conversation began, the old gentleman always got round to talking about Sir George Crewe. Sir George died in 1844, but Arthur Kirkman was old enough to have vivid memories of him. He regarded Sir George as a saint and was never tired of talking about him.

There is no doubt in my mind, that of all the baronets of Calke, Sir George was by far the most outstanding, and it is important to know something of his background.

He inherited the title and estates as 8th baronet in 1819 at the age of twenty four, following the untimely death of his father Sir Henry, who was killed in a coaching accident in London. Sir George's grandfather, Sir Harry, was known as the sporting baronet for whom the most important things in life were shooting, racing and coursing. Although he never won any of the major races, he was, like his father before him, an enthusiastic breeder of racehorses. The horse were trained, not at Calke, where the ground was unsuitable, but at Swarkeston, where racing stables were established. Sir Harry spent little on Calke Abbey but began the work of landscaping the park which was to be continued by his son. His worldliness must have been the despair of his wife, Lady Frances Harpur, whom, as Lady Frances Greville, daughter of the Earl of Warwick, he had married in 1762. In complete contrast to her husband, she was a deeply religious person, noted for her evangelical piety, who regarded this life with all its trials and tribulations as a preparation for the next. She espoused the Methodist cause, associated herself with the Countess of Huntingdon's chapels, and eventually became a member of the Moravian Church. It must have been deeply wounding to her to have to tolerate her husband's way of life and lack of religion. He died in 1789 at the age of fifty, 'without', she wrote sadly, 'a thought for Eternity'.

If Lady Frances had hoped that her son Henry who succeeded as 7th baronet, might bring some credit to the family and cause her less sorrow by his behaviour, she was to be sadly disillusioned. Sir Henry, who was to become known as the isolated baronet, although conscious of his position as an important landowner, cared little for society or for convention, and although he came out of his seclusion to serve his term as sheriff for the county, and to take command of the Derbyshire Volunteer Cavalry, which had been formed to meet the threat of invasion from Revolutionary France, once that emergency was over, he retreated once more into his shell. At Calke, he constructed an entrance drive south of the park, with a stone bridge over the Calke valley, so it was

Sir George Crewe, with his son John.

said, that he could drive off to London unobserved by the inhabitants of either Melbourne or Ashby-de-la-Zouch! The bridge and part of the drive have disappeared under the Staunton Harold reservoir, but what remains is still known as Sir Henry's Lane. He built the underground tunnel from the gardens at Calke so that the gardeners going to and from their work could not be seen from the Pleasure Grounds. Sir Henry also built the entrance lodges to the park, and at the Abbey itself, remodelled the principal rooms, adding the library, although I have never forgiven him for adding the entrance portico. I am not alone in considering that this addition, although no doubt fashionable at the time, detracts from the appearance of the south front. Some years ago during my time as agent, the authors of a proposed book on country house architecture were given permission to photograph Calke, and I was interested to note that they ignored the south front, remarking that it had been spoilt by Sir Henry Harpur. After completing his work at Calke, Sir Henry decreed, no doubt harking back to its monastic origin, that Calke House or Calke Hall as it was then called, should be known in future as Calke Abbey, a title to which it has no real claim. It would have been more correct to have renamed it Calke Priory.

In 1790, his mother Lady Frances was distressed to learn that her son had taken a mistress. a lady's maid known as Nanny Hawkins who had been installed in a house near Calke Park. When they married in 1792 and Nanny Hawkins arrived at Calke as Lady Harpur, Georgian society was outraged. Taking a mistress was commonplace, and could have been overlooked, but marriage to the lady flouted all convention. The pious Lady Frances however, who was far more concerned with morality than with convention, took a different view. In coming to terms with the situation, she discovered that although the new Lady Harpur had been only a lady's maid, she had otherwise much to recommend her and in all, seemed relieved that the marriage had brought to an end an immoral relationship. Lady Harpur's early days at Calke may have been difficult and we do not know how she was received, but from a statement that Sir Henry 'would not suffer any man, friend or servant to see his wife', he appears to have kept her apart, at any rate in the early days.

Lady Frances, having become reconciled with the situation, tried to keep in contact with the family at Calke, but as time went on, her evangelical piety and attempts to reform her son, about whom she remarked 'he has no religion and does not even go to church', probably drove him to the point of distraction, and he finally forbade her to visit the family, either at Calke or his town house in London.

For the remainder of his life, Sir Henry, having turned his back on society, became increasingly isolated. He had no direct contact with the servants and dined alone, not even allowing a servant to wait on him. In view of this isolation, it is somewhat surprising that he should have coveted a peerage, and this can perhaps only be explained in terms of character contradictions which were something of a tradition in the family. Sir Henry, always conscious of his wealth and importance as one of the largest landowners in the county, must have felt that this merited something more than a baronetcy, the lowest rank of hereditary title, with no seat on the House of Lords. No doubt with this in mind he petitioned to have the dormant barony of Crewe revived in his favour, through descent from his great great grandmother Catherine Crewe who was one of the co-heiresses of Lord Crewe of Steane.

Probably in anticipation of becoming a peer and to assist in his claim, he incorporated the Crewe arms with those of Harpur, the Crewe motto 'Degeneranti genus approbrium' replacing the Harpur 'Cogita mori.' He also adopted the name of Crewe itself, so that the family name became Harpur Crewe. The claim failed but it is interesting to note that over the succeeding years, the name Harpur tended to disappear from general use in favour of Crewe, except on official documents and family memorials. During my early years, members of the family were always referred to as Crewes, and the property as the Crewe estates. The name Harpur was never used and did not come back into use until Charles Jenney, who inherited the estates from his aunt, Mrs. Mosley, changed his name to Harpur Crewe to comply with her wish. When Sir Henry was killed in the coaching accident in 1819 he was succeeded by his eldest son George as 8th baronet.

The contrast between father and son could not have been more pronounced. As a young man with a social conscience and strong sense of duty, guided by the highest Christian moral principles, Sir George entered upon his inheritance with 'a mixture of painful and pleasurable emotions'. He was overwhelmed by the sheer size of Calke Abbey and wrote in his diary: 'I cannot say its size makes me feel proud, but rather shrink within myself in deep humility'. There is no doubt that Sir George inherited these ideals from his grandmother, and the bond between them that had been broken when she was banned from Calke was renewed after his father's death. To Sir George, the inheritance of a large estate was a privilege which carried a heavy responsibility, and he proceeded to devote the rest of his life to the welfare of his tenants, all his actions being based on his high moral standards of Christian charity and strict propriety. In this he was to set the hallmark of stewardship of the land which was to become the pattern for succeeding generations of the family.

Upon his succession, following his father's very different regime, there was much to rectify, and at the outset there was an immediate change in the moral climate at Calke with daily prayers for the family and servants, and strict Sunday observance becoming a household rule. It was a daunting task, but in due course he was able to say that 'under God's blessing, after 19 years of labours, I have at last cleansed the Augaean stables of Calke jobs, Calke turkey and Calke extravagance'. His grandmother Lady Frances must have viewed all this with the greatest satisfaction. She lived until 1825, long enough to see her grandson with the situation firmly under control. It is fitting that her portrait by the artist Tilly Kettle, should have pride of place amongst the family portraits in the Saloon at Calke.

The extensive estate in the moorlands of North Staffordshire had been largely ignored by successive generations of the family, apart from its value for sporting, but Sir George became concerned about the backward state of the area, and the conditions in which his tenants were living. He decided that with so much requiring attention, occasional visits were of little use, and he built Warslow Hall as a residence so that he could stay for longer periods to plan and supervise the improvements which he put in hand. Although he employed an agent, he took a personal interest in all that was taking place, both here and at Calke.

Sir George did not undertake any major re-construction of Calke Abbey, but he put the house into proper repair, altering the entrance hall and gave the Saloon its moulded ceiling. He also purchased some pictures, notable paintings of horses by James Ward and John Ferneley, and commissioned some landscapes of Calke Park by John Glover. In 1826 he remodelled Calke Church.

It is not surprising that Sir George was in the forefront of the move for universal education. Before the Education Act of 1876 made schooling compulsory, and a national responsibility, most education in the first half of the nineteenth century was provided by religious organisations, and of these the National Society for promoting the education of the poor in the principles of the Church of England, was the established church's answer to the non-comformists' British and Foreign Schools Society. As a member of the established church it was the former that would naturally commend itself to Sir George. At Twyford he gave land for the erection of the village school where I received my primary education, and elsewhere on his estates he gave land for this purpose and often helped financially with the erection of the school itself. In North Staffordshire this would often go hand in hand with the building of a church, sometimes under the same roof. At Ticknall in 1842, he was instrumental, largely at his own expense, in the building of the parish church of St. George to replace the old church of St. Thomas a Becket, The new church which stands near the ruins of the old, is dedicated to the patron saint of England, but it is said that it is really dedicated to Sir George Crewe of Calke. If this is so we can only commend the wishes of the parishioners to pay tribute in this way to a remarkable man. Near the Ticknall entrance to Calke Park he built a school for girls which he placed under the control of Lady Crewe and became known as Lady Crewe's Free School. It was here that four of my great-aunts, members of the Hudson family, were educated.

Sir George's social conscience and sense of duty was not confined to his own estates. He entered into public life, serving as Sheriff of Derbyshire in 1821. During his term. he discontinued the traditional Assize Ball, on the grounds that it was "unseemly for ladies and gentlemen to amuse themselves, on the eve of the day on which others were to be on trial for their lives". Later on, in 1827, he refused to subscribe to a plate to be raced for by the Derbyshire Yeomanry, because he thought it would encourage betting amongst working men, some of whom were his tenants, to the neglect of their proper duties. He regarded horse racing as a menace.

Sir George hated politics. because, he said "they involve all the bitterness, the rancour, the prejudice of party: could it be possible for all persons to unite as Christians ought to do, for the public weal, I should then delight in them as cordially as I now detest them. To labour for the public good is — and I trust always will be — the greatest delight of my life". It was therefore, only out of a sense of duty, that he agreed to stand for parliament for South Derbyshire in 1821 when "the Tory interest in Derbyshire was apparently lost without hope of recovery". He served until 1835, when ill health forced him to resign.

As a fairminded person, Sir George supported the Reform Bill of 1832, but opposed the harsh Game Laws, which he said he could no longer enforce as a magistrate. He objected to the large estates practice of game rearing, as he said, this only encouraged poaching.

If Sir George had not inherited Calke he would have been happy to live the life of a farmer, and had in fact expressed this wish to his father. It is not surprising therefore, to find that he took an active interest in his farm at Calke. From his diary we note that on July 13th 1832, he was working with a party in the hayfield. "We got up to 10 or 12 loads in very good order". In that year he bought 30 Polled Galloways and 20 Ayrshire heifers at Red Hill near Nottingham. In 1835 he travelled to the Isle of Portland to purchase Portland sheep from the foundation flock there.

To his tenants, Sir George was a fair and benevolent landlord, but he was also a realist. When he inherited Calke. he found the rental showing many tenants in unacceptable arrears, and had no hesitation in sending them a stern letter saying that this state of affairs must cease. He pointed out that the rents were reasonable, and that he was always prepared to grant indulgence in the case of genuine distress. but if a tenant was incapable of managing his farm, or was living beyond his means, it would be better for him to give up the tenancy before running further into debt.

Throughout his life Sir George suffered from ill health, which makes it all the more remarkable that he was able to achieve so much. He regarded himself as accountable to Almighty God for all his actions, and in the light of this would examine his conduct before retiring at the end of each day. He recorded the day's events in his diary with meticulous care, and from these we can see the extent to which he knew his tenants personally, and his concern for their health and welfare. My own family recall his concern when my great grandfather's brother William Hudson lost his life in the double drowning tragedy in Calke Park in 1840, the story of which has been told elsewhere. Sir George took personal charge of the search for the missing boys. Sir George's other writings are of a philosophical nature, showing his concern for matters troubling his own and the nation's conscience.

He died in 1844 after a short illness at the early age of 48, and his agent wrote in his diary: 'There was lost to his friends and dependents the most kind and benevolent man that ever lived'. Over a thousand mourners attended his funeral at Calke on the 9th of January. His obituary in the Derby Mercury shows the esteem in which he was held, even when allowance is made for the somewhat extravagant language of the time, and contrasts noticeably with the matter of fact way in which his father's death had been reported in 1819, when no reference was made to the character of the deceased. You can see a portrait of Sir George with his infant son John in the Saloon at Calke, not far from that of his grandmother Lady Frances.

The stained glass east window in Calke Church is in his memory where you can also see an illustration of the diamond shaped seal of the Peculiar of Calke, the original of which is in the Abbey. This seal designated the church as a 'Peculiar', i.e, not under the control of the bishop.

Tribute to Sir George Crewe —
Derby Mercury 3 January 1844

With deep and sincere regret we announce in our obituary of this day the death of Sir George Crewe Bart, of Calke Abbey, a man whose truly Christian character, whose comprehension and untiring benevolence and whose unspotted private and unimpeachable public life, have made him honoured and beloved by all around him.

The death of such a man as Sir George Crewe is no common event. It creates a void not easily filled. Connected as the Hon. Baronet was with the many religious and civil institutions which adorn the land, and to which he was most anxious to render most effective support by his contribution at all times, and by his personal advocacy of their particular merits, whenever his health permitted him to engage in public affairs, and to take part in the proceedings of public meetings — firm and unchanging in his attachment to our constitution in Church and State — equally so to the cause of the poor, to whatever might tend to their temporal and spiritual benefit, and on whose behalf an appeal to his liberality was never made in vain — and holding a position in the county by which his influence was extensively and beneficially exercised, his death may well be regarded as a general loss, the effect of which must be severely felt amongst all classes, and in every relation of society. We do not wish to speak in terms of mere eulogy, but is impossible to refer with any degree of justice to the character of Sir George Crewe, without using language that in itself partakes of the panegyrical. We are convinced that we do but give utterance to the feelings of our readers and the public at large to whom Sir George was known, either personally or from report when we say, that a more estimable man, or devout Christian, than was the Hon. Baronet, it would be difficult to name.

Chapter Thirteen
Sir John Crewe

SIR JOHN, educated at Rugby and Trinity College, Cambridge, succeeded to the title and estates at the age of twenty. The following year he married his cousin, Georgiana Henrietta Eliza, the second daughter of Vice Admiral W. Stanhope Lovell at the fashionable London Church of St. George's, Hanover Square.

There was general rejoicing amongst the tenantry, and dinners were given in honour of the bride and bridegroom. Sir John must have felt the burden of succeeding a father who had been so revered, and it is interesting to note that at a dinner given at Longnor by the North Staffordshire tenants, the proposer of the toast to the bride and bridegroom, said more by way of tribute to the bridegroom's late father than to the groom himself. Sir John does not however, appear to have been adversely affected by this adulation of his father. A man of kindly and generous disposition, if he lacked the energy and reforming zeal of Sir George, he had no intention of departing from the tradition established by his father, and throughout his life was content to fulfil the role he had inherited, and came close to becoming the ideal of a benevolent 19th century landowner. Apart from serving his term as Sheriff in 1853, he took little part in public affairs, being content to occupy his time with the daily routine that the possession of large estates demanded. Sir John was interested in natural history and added to the collection at Calke, but his main interest was farming, particularly the breeding of Longhorn cattle and Portland sheep on the home farm, and he was a major prize winner at the leading agricultural shows. The cattle were kept at Standleys Barn Farm which adjoins the park, and there the doors of the sheds where they were housed had been widened, to accommodate the long horns which are characteristic of the breed. At that time, the object of cattle breeding was to increase the size of the animals, and landowners and farmers vied with each other to produce the largest specimens. Artists were employed to paint the prizewinners, who would exaggerate the proportions of the animals to please their patrons. Examples of this can be seen at Calke, together with the mounted heads of prizewinning animals in the Entrance Hall.

Sir John carried out major improvements to the farms and cottages on his estates, and encouraged his tenants, with whom he was always on the best of terms, to adopt high standards. He was a pioneer in the making of silage, being one of the first to construct a special pit for this purpose, the remains of which can still be seen near the home farm. During his time the Calke lands developed the prosperous and well ordered appearance recalled by my grandfather Herbert Cox. This personal relationship with the tenants became part of Calke's tradition, and would extend to others connected with the estate. The Harpur Crewes were on good terms with the Boswell family of gypsies, who were allowed to camp at Calke. One member of the family, Delilah Boswell, who sold clothes pegs from door to door, was a particular favourite. She was always welcome to call at Calke Abbey, and on one occasion, agreed to be taken to a studio to be photographed. When she died in 1885, aged 85 years of age, she was buried in Ticknall

Sir John Crewe.

churchyard where for some years afterwards, following Romany tradition, members of her family would gather to sing hymns at the graveside. Her grave can still be seen, marked by a simple Celtic iron cross, which over the years was maintained by the Harpur Crewes.

Towards the end of his life, Sir John, who had always been somewhat reserved, retired more and more from contact with his fellow men, until he became virtually a recluse. This did not mean that he confined himself to Calke Abbey however, but would often ride off on horseback, alone over his vast acres, speaking to no one, sometimes not returning until nightfall. His death in 1886, after being owner of Calke for 42 years, was universally lamented, and a great crowd of mourners attended his funeral. Henry Forman, one of the tenants from the nearby village of Chellaston recorded in his diary. 'Sat. 6th March 1886. This morning I went to Calke Abbey to attend the funeral of the late Sir J. H. Crewe Bart. He was buried in a vault in Calke Church. The wreaths were most beautiful and numerous, quite covering the coffin.

There were three coffins. The first was of cedar grown on the estate and lined with quilted white satin, the body enveloped in cashmere; the second was lead, and the third oak, made out of a tree cut down in the park, a thousand years old. The furniture was silver plated and very massive costing £40, the pall of best silk velvet with silver lace and fringe costing £60.

Sir John was succeeded by his eldest son Vauncey who was destined to be the last baronet of Calke.

Delilah Boswell.

Chapter Fourteen
Sir Vauncey Crewe

SIR VAUNCEY, who succeeded in 1886, was cast in an entirely different mould. Born in 1846 and named after a mediaeval ancestor, he was educated privately at Calke, attending neither school nor university, and this in itself may have contributed to a naturally reclusive nature. Owner of some 12,000 acres in Derbyshire and Lord of fifteen manors apart from extensive property in the uplands of North Staffordshire, Sir Vauncey was monarch of all he surveyed, and ruling over this vast empire on his behalf was his agent John Shaw of Derby.

From an early date, Sir Vauncey turned his back, not only on society in general, but on almost everybody in particular, to devote a lifetime to shooting and the collection of natural history specimens to add to the collection at Calke Abbey.

Unlike his father, he had little or no interest in farming, even though his income depended entirely on it. Sir John, who would have been aware of this, left instructions for the livestock to be sold after his death. Thus the herd of long horned cattle was dispersed, and all but a small number of the Portland sheep.

Under Sir Vauncey's regime, the estate became a vast game preserve, where tenants were forbidden to cut and lay the hedges or to drain the land, and an army of gamekeepers was employed to preserve the game and keep the poachers at bay. I remember my grandfather, Herbert Cox, who could recall those days, telling me that after Sir John's death, it was noticeable how rapidly the neat and well ordered appearance of the countryside changed, like 'a once well tended garden where the gardener had departed'. Lord Norton, Sir Vauncey's father-in-law noted in his diary after a visit to Calke in 1890: 'To Calke Abbey. In this magnificent park 'Lady Catherine's Bower', a relic of life gone out. Steps and bridge over valley and water, to sylvan retreat where ladies sat and men idled while a musician played. Now the whole place given over to game preserves, and not even drained, that the rushes may give cover'.

I remember some thirty years after Sir Vauncey's death, the tenancy of a farm was changing hands and the estate valuer was carrying out the usual inspection on the farm to make a claim for dilapidations against the outgoing tenant, for items which were not being left in proper condition according to the rules of good husbandry. All the hedges were overgrown and neglected, and when this was pointed out to the tenant, he produced a letter from Sir Vauncey forbidding him to touch any of the hedges on the farm! In fact overgrown hedges anywhere came to be known as 'Sir Vauncey' hedges.

One of the few guests to stay at Calke Abbey in those days was Lady Crewe's brother Father Adderley, son of Lord Norton. The Rt. Hon Sir Charles Bowyer Adderley, first Baron Norton, has been described as a kindly Christian gentleman and a high minded statesman. Although a conservative in name, he had served as conservative member of parliament for North Staffordshire for 37 years until his elevation to the peerage in

1878, he was a reformer by nature. Entirely devoid of self-seeking, he did much to alleviate the social conditions of the time. A man of deep religious convictions, the whole of his life and work was set against this background. In character he may be likened to Sir George Crewe of Calke.

As an M.P. and President of the Board of Trade, he developed an interest in the colonies, particularly New Zealand. The family seat was Hams Hall, near Birmingham, and Lord Norton recalled that many of his ideas were formed walking up and down on the terrace at Hams. The Hams Treaty with the Maoris, and the Constitution of New Zealand were in fact, formulated there.

Lord Norton died in 1905 aged 90 years. After the Adderleys left Hams, the house was taken down and re-erected (minus the ground floor) to become one of the Halls of Residence of the Royal Agricultural College at Cirencester. Hams Hall Power Station was later built on the site.

Fr. James Adderley was one of two sons of Lord Norton who took Holy Orders. His brother Reginald became Vicar of Chesterfield in Derbyshire. Educated at Eton and Oxford, James left with little academic distinction but with an honourable reputation. In his early days as a priest he worked in London's East End where, with two fellow priests he founded the Society of Divine Compassion, a community following the Franciscan rule. Although Fr. Adderley appeared to have little understanding of the economic problems of the time, the humanitarian aspect of socialism appealed to him, and he developed left wing views. He was concerned about what he regarded as intolerable conditions in society, and found a place in his heart for the outcasts and downtrodden. In character, he was however, probably little different from his sister Lady Crewe, who was equally concerned with those less well placed than herself. Brother and sister operated against very different backgrounds.

As a member of the aristocracy — he was the son of a wealthy peer, and entitled to use the title of "honourable", which he never used, — he was an "odd man out" who cared little for material possessions, nor indeed, much about his personal appearance.

When James formed an Anglican brotherhood under vows, following an almost monk-like existence, Lord Norton, an orthodox churchman. who had little sympathy with vows of celibacy, became concerned, and consulted Archbishop Benson. The Archbishop made enquiries, and was able to tell Lord Norton that all was well, and the brother's simple life among the poor was fulfiling a deep need of the time. Lord Norton was reassured but remarked to a friend when James became known as Father Adderley: 'I draw the line at calling my son "Father".'

In 1904 Fr. Adderley was appointed Vicar of St. Saviour's Saltley, a suburb of Birmingham, a church which Lord Norton had built. The Adderleys owned land there, which was being developed for housing. In 1911 he was appointed to St. Gabriel's, Birmingham, and in 1918 returned to London.

A powerful preacher, Fr. Adderley could fill a church to overflowing, and on occasions a marquee had to be erected to contain the crowd. On visits to Calke, he would preach in Ticknall Church to a packed congregation, and one one occasion, with Sir Vauncey sitting in his pew below, denounced the wealthy landowners, stating that, in his opinion, it was only a matter of time before they were abolished. How Sir Vauncey managed to tolerate Fr. Adderley's presence at Calke it is difficult to imagine!

As the years went by, Sir Vauncey became increasingly isolated from those around him, apart from Agathos (Agg) Pegg, his head gamekeeper, who became his only close

Photo by Elliot & Fry

Right Hon. Sir C. B. Adderley, K.C.M.G., First Lord Norton.

The Terrace at Hams, where the Constitution of New Zealand was planned.

Father Adderley.

confidant and friend. Lady Crewe whom as the Hon. Isabel Adderley, the youngest daughter of the first Lord Norton, Sir Vauncey had married in 1876, was a highly intelligent person who had little in common with her husband, and they appear to have led almost separate lives. Throughout her life, Lady Crewe upheld the Calke tradition of concern for the welfare of employees and tenants on the estate, Sir Vauncey having abdicated his responsibilities in this direction. When Lady Crewe received visitors at Calke, Sir Vauncey would not meet them, and would leave the house before they arrived, not returning until he was sure they had left. At Calke he had virtually no contact with the staff; in fact the servants were instructed to go out of their way to avoid him. Thus the maids were told that if they were in one of the corridors and heard his footsteps, they were to disappear into the nearest room until he had passed by. One maid claimed that in the two years she was in service at Calke, she never saw Sir Vauncey.

Over the years he continued to add to the natural history collection at Calke, until room after room was filled with specimens, and days when the weather prevented him going out on the estate collecting, would be spent in the house, recording and cataloguing. When conditions made it necessary, he had fires in the rooms to maintain an even temperature, and woebetide the maid who let a fire go out, or built one up too high. If this happened he would write a note to the housekeeper, ordering the maid to be dismissed. In fact no sacking ever took place. Lady Crewe always stood between Sir Vauncey and the worst of his eccentricities, and never allowed this to happen. Presumably, since he did not know one servant from another, he thought his order had been carried out, and another maid had taken her place. On servant who was a cook in the early 1920s told me that while she was at Calke there was a coal strike, and not even Sir Vauncey could obtain a supply of coal. She had great difficulty in cooking on the stove in the old kitchen with wet wood which was supplied as fuel, and was 'sacked,' several times by Sir Vauncey, for under or overcooking the chicken he always had for lunch. Over dinner in the servants' hall, the standing joke was — "Who has been sacked today?"

The river Trent flowed through the estate. At one time the river had been navigated using horse drawn barges, but this had ceased by the beginning of the nineteenth century, to become once more a quiet watercourse where Sir Vauncey jealously guarded the fishing and wildfowling. One can imagine his consternation when, early in 1887, it came to his notice that an attempt was to made by a company called the Upper Trent Navigation Company, to open up the river for steam navigation by means of a Parliamentary Bill. An outraged Sir Vauncey immediately instructed John Shaw to call a meeting of all the other landowners concerned, and to mount the strongest possible opposition to the Bill. The correspondence between owner and agent, on heavily black edged notepaper, being within the year following his father's death, has been preserved and gives an interesting insight into the way Sir Vauncey thought and acted.

In January 1887 he wrote to John Shaw, saying that he had had second thoughts about accepting his advice to allow the promoters to carry out an initial survey. He writes 'I wish they (the promoters) were at the bottom of the Trent and I would not mind telling them so'. After this he ordered my great-grandfather John Hudson, and the other gamekeepers along the river, to patrol the banks with shotguns to keep the Company's surveyors away so as to prevent the initial survey taking place.

Opposite: Sir Vauncey Crewe.

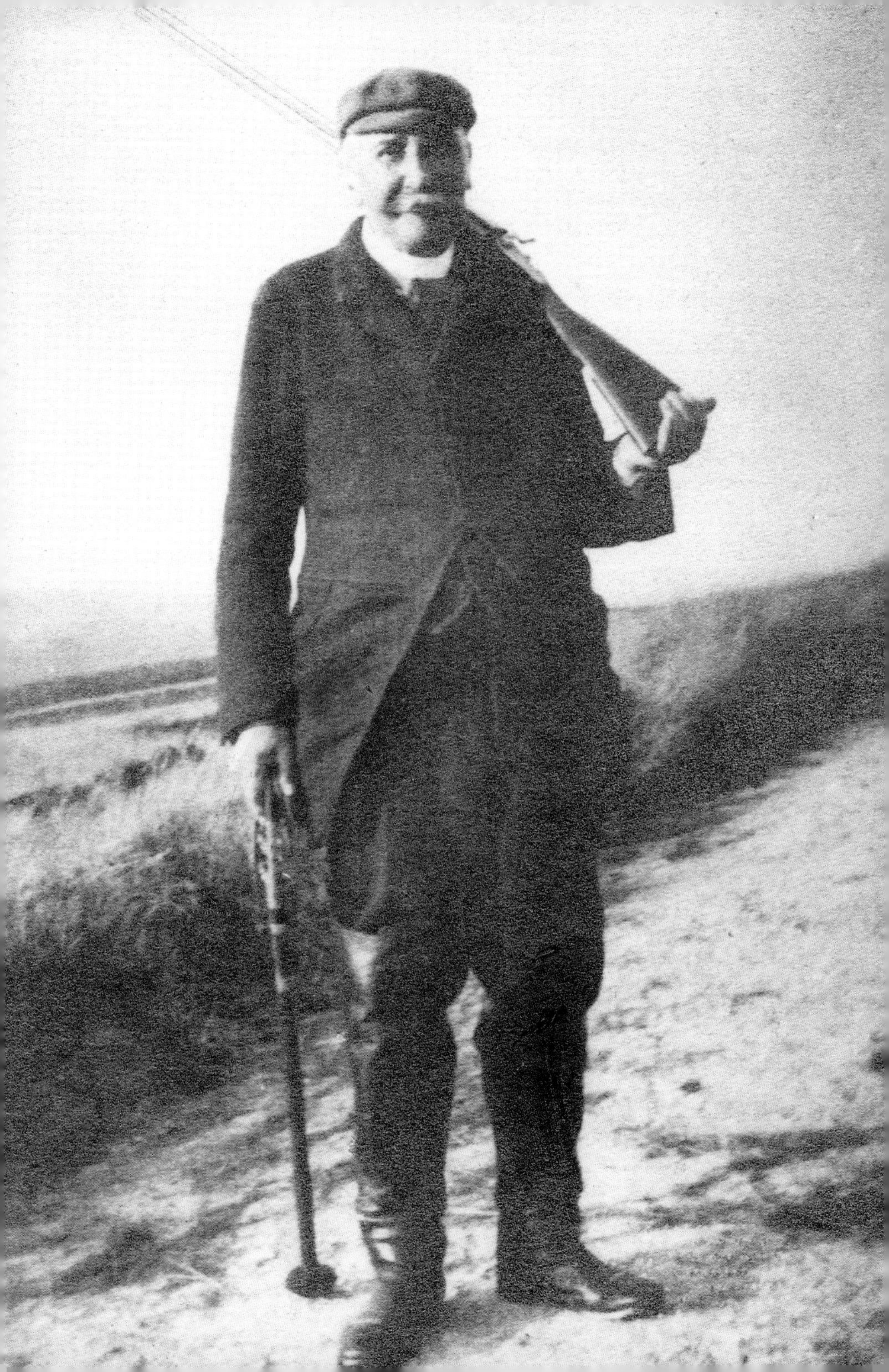

In a further letter to Mr. Shaw, Sir Vauncey points out that the bed of the river belongs to the Lord of the Manor, and 'they ask for powers to dredge it for steam navigation — what does this mean? It means turning the river into a vast highway, utterly destroying the fishing and wildlife shooting, destroying the spawning beds of the fish and their natural food, and leaving no nesting place for the wildfowl either by day or night. The steamers in a narrow river like the Trent would stir up all the mud from Burton, and silt the river up over and over again, and the filthy smoke from the funnels would destroy the vegetation far and wide stretching to Foremark and even Calke. Boat loads of excursionists would come up and down, armed with guns, nets and walking stick guns, and be here, there and everywhere, it would be impossible to stop them. We ought to have the right to search all steamers and boats for guns and nets, and even then we could no longer preserve the Trent — it would be quite useless.

River police would be required to preserve law and order and should be paid for by the Company and extra police would be required on the ground as well. What does the Company want with a towing path? They don't want steam AND Towing paths surely. In that case they would have two highways through my estate instead of one. The towing path would be lined with fishermen and guns out of the large towns who would set us completely at defiance, and boatloads of excursionists could land where and whenever they chose and penetrate to Foremark and Calke and spread all over the ground right and left of the Trent. A nice lot they would be too, out of all the large towns, Nottingham. Birmingham, Derby, Burton. Stoke and Newark. I don't care what the engineers say, the Trent is a queer river — I like deeds not words. I will believe them when they have accomplished their work, not before. If they deepen the river too much, it is quite possible they will leave us high and dry in hot seasons. nothing but stagnant pools full of Burton sewage, all the water or a good deal of it run off to the sea. I am quite certain the steamers will wash down the banks and undermine the walls in no time, especially in flood time, and deepening the river will increase the strength of the current. The Trent meadows with overdrainage will be as bad as too many floods on it, it will be worth very little. The steamers will drive all the salmon out of the river and entirely prevent fishing either by rod or net. Speaking for myself alone, I say that the Company could not compensate me for all I should lose in every way. Of course we are the only real opponents, the Confiscation Bill concerns the landowners and no-one else much. It is not required. There are two lines of railway and a canal through my estate to Burton — what more do they want? This should be mentioned, also that some engineers went round to my tenants and tried to persuade them to sign a paper in favour of the scheme and when they refused to do so, said they would have their way in spite of Sir Vauncey and his tenants. If this Bill is passed by the present Conservative government, I shall not support them in the future, nor shall I keep foxes either side of the Trent for the Burton and Derby contingents to ride after. I am quite determined about this. I don't see why our property should be confiscated for the benefit of the towns and the Company. In the case of war with a foreign power, if this scheme is carried out, it would be necessary to fortify the mouth of the Trent and Humber, otherwise there would be nothing to prevent the gun and torpedo boats of the enemy from coming all the way up and laying waste all the large towns in ashes throughout the centre of England which now they could not do!' Sir Vauncey then goes on 'hope a bold front will be shown all along the line'. Ever mindful of costs however, he states 'All expenses should be carefully kept down in connection with this affair, and the case carefully watched so that we are not led on too far with regard to money.' One can imagine Sir Vauncey's delight when in due course he heard that the Bill had been defeated, and the river Trent was to be allowed to continue to meander peacefully through his estate.

As the years passed by Sir Vauncey became increasingly eccentric and difficult and some of his actions became alarming in their consequences.

One example of this concerned the fate of Repton Park, a large house on the estate, some six miles from Calke. Sir Vauncey's cousin, Edmund Crewe lived there, and they were not on the best of terms. One day Sir Vauncey decided to go to Repton Park with Agg Pegg, in search of butterflies for the Calke collection. On arrival they parked the pony and trap in the drive, and without making a courtesy call on the tenant, proceeded to march across the lawn into the shrubbery complete with butterfly nets. They were, however, promptly challenged by Edmund Crewe who by then had appeared at the front door. 'What do you think you are doing?' he demanded, to which Sir Vauncey replied: 'I think I can do as I like on my own property: go back into the house, I will deal with you later'. Sir Vauncey then abandoned the search for butterflies and returned to Calke in a rage. On arrival he sent for John Shaw his agent and gave instructions for Repton Park to be demolished. Accordingly a few days later, a procession of carts and waggons with men and tackle left Ticknall for Repton and proceeded to demolish the house stone by stone. Before the demolition began John Shaw, the agent, asked Sir Vauncey what was to be done with the furniture in the house, to which he replied: 'The furniture belongs to my cousin. Make a pile of it on the lawn, he can do what he likes with it'. As the result of all this, the unfortunate Mr. Crewe was obliged to seek refuge in a farmhouse in the nearby village of Milton, where he remained until the end of his days. Today all that remains is the landscaped park with the entrance gates, and avenue of trees leading to the site, but of the house itself nothing remains save a fragment of the cellars or undercroft, to bear silent witness to Sir Vauncey's folly.

If that was how Sir Vauncey treated his cousin, he was capable of dealing just as severely with members of his own family. He was not on good terms with one of his daughters Airmyne Crewe; in fact they did not speak to each other and communicated by letters sent through the post! Sir Vauncey was always afraid of fire, to the point that it became an obsession and he lived in constant fear of Calke Abbey burning down, and with it his natural history collection. Every night before retiring himself, he would pace the corridors until the small hours of the morning, checking the rooms to make sure that the last embers of the numerous fires were out. For this reason, smoking was forbidden, and one day he had reason to suspect that Airmyne was smoking in defiance of his orders. Pegg was ordered to check on her. He discovered that it was so, but did not report to her father. Soon afterwards, however, Sir Vauncey was in his room when cigarette smoke drifted in through the window from Airmyne's room below. Rushing down stairs he caught her redhanded and ordered her to leave Calke immediately. He provided a pony and trap to take her into Derby, where she sought refuge with friends. Shortly afterwards she left the district and never returned to Calke during her father's lifetime. I suspect, however, there was more to the story than that.

If the tenanted land on the estate became virtually a game preserve with an army of gamekeepers to control the tenants and keep poachers at bay, Calke Park itself, where there were no tenants to control, was under even greater surveillance and here Sir Vauncey's rule was absolute. Nothing was permitted to disturb the wildlife, and for this reason motor cars were banned. The few visitors to the house who arrived by car had to leave their vehicles at one of the lodges and complete the journey through the park by pony and trap which Sir Vauncey provided. This rule applied to his son Richard Crewe who, although he owned a motor car, had no special dispensation.

Sir Vauncey's interest in farming was minimal, and although the agricultural rents were his main source of income, he seemed to regard the activities of his farming tenants as a threat to his own interests. The depression which followed the first World War when farms became vacant and it was difficult to find new tenants, resulted in some of the farms being taken in hand, to be run by the landlord. This gave Sir Vauncey a greater degree of control over the sporting interest, but with the continued agricultural depression. a situation made worse by some of the bailiffs who took advantage of their position, a state of affairs was reached which could not continue, and when Lady Crewe asked to see the farming accounts she declared that 'if that was farming, in future the farms must be let at any price'. After this, no more farms were taken in hand, and in some cases where a farm which became vacant was in a poor state due to the failure or neglect of the tenant, it would be let rent free for a period, to enable the incoming tenant to put things in order and survive.

Sir Vauncey's obsession with sporting and natural history continued unabated for the whole of his life, and his gamekeepers were always on the lookout for rare birds to add to his collection. At Calke Abbey, room after room became filled with specimens which he had either collected on the estate, or purchased at sales, until over thirty rooms were filled to over flowing, representing a lifetime's work of this remarkable eccentric.

Sir Vauncey died in 1924, having outlived his only son and heir Richard Fynderne Harpur Crewe. Richard was in character completely different from his father. With a scientific turn of mind, besides being a keen motorist he was interested in ships and aeroplanes, in fact in all the latest inventions. In 1911. Richard took a flight in an aeroplane, and wrote an account of the experience, for the benefit of readers of the Ticknall Church magazine.

Gamekeepers, with the dogs, gathered outside Calke Abbey in 1887. John Hudson, the author's great-grandfather is fourth from the right.

A FLIGHT ON A FLYING MACHINE.
R. F. H. Crewe

A few weeks ago having been fortunate enough in getting a flight on a flying machine, or, to speak more correctly, an aeroplane, I have been asked if I would give some account of my experience to readers of this magazine, who, though familiar with the sight of these machines, either by pictures in the illustrated papers, or possibly from what they saw at Burton last year, do not know what it feels like to be actually travelling through the air.

The following is a short account of a flight I made recently as a passenger. Having previously arranged with a clever French aviator, Monsieur Ducrocq, who was once a pupil of Paulhan, the man who flew from London to Manchester, to have a flight directly a day was suitable, I went to the big flying ground at Brooklands, near London, to see if the conditions were satisfactory. When I met Monsieur Ducrocq he said, "At present there is too much wind; towards evening it may drop." So whilst waiting I inspected the numerous aeroplanes in the sheds there, it being one of the places where flying is taught. As time wore on, the wind went down considerably, and several machines came out, making flights though the weather was uncertain, and one aeroplane in coming down too suddenly, was wrecked, but the driver (or pilot as he is called) had a marvellous escape, being uninjured. Another less experienced flyer also alighted rapidly, the engine of his machine having stopped, he nearly fell into the river, but escaped with a broken wing! It was nearly sunset when my French aviator wheeled his machine out of its shed, a large aeroplane called a racing Farman bi-plane, with an engine of 50 horse-power. After taking the aeroplane on a short trial flight, he said all was ready, and told me to empty my pockets of all loose things, in case they dropped out and got amongst the machinery, which would have been disastrous. Pulling my cap well down over my ears, I carefully climbed up into the tiny seat at the back of the driver, a very cramped position amongst numerous wires and woodwork. My pilot was sitting almost between my knees, his right hand holding the controlling lever — woe-betide jogging his elbow: any decided movement would upset the balance and down we should both come! "What is your weight?" "I told him. "Now, are you ready? we shall feel some motion". "Yes," said I. A low whistle and the engine is started — a loud roar as the propeller increases speed. The signal to "Let go" is given and we rush down the ground like a racing motor car. Almost before I realize it we are off the ground; looking down I see we already twenty or thirty feet up, and getting higher every second; the speed of the machine increases to fifty miles per hour, the rush of the air past you is terrific, feeling as though it is being driven through you, and intensely cold. My first sensation is one of complete security, the machine at the time forging ahead, more like a huge battleship than anything else; then a puff of wind comes and we roll slowly, but quite unlike a ship. However, we soon steady down again, and fly out over the heads of the people far below; you can see them gazing up as you pass. On we fly down the ground, by the great motor racing track. Then we turn, heeling over considerably as the corner is taken, meeting the wind which makes the machine almost stagger, but once round we increase speed again, the driver in front steadying the aeroplane with his lever. On looking over your shoulder, close to the seat, you see the shadowy form of the great screw-propeller whizzing round at one thousand revolutions to the minute, making the wire rigging tremble with the vibrations, but you feel none of this. We are now crossing a sewerage farm, a veritable trap for unlucky aeroplanes. I hope we don't make a hasty descent here! But we keep flying steadily on, past the aviation sheds, the sun rapidly sinking and dusk falling. After flying some ten miles we circle out over the river and rise slightly higher, then prepare to descend. The engine is stopped, the aeroplane is allowed to dive straight to the earth, but just as you think you must hit it heavily, the controlling lever is moved, the engine restarts, and the machine goes on an even course once again a foot or so above the ground, finally gliding gently to earth. The flight is over.

It is impossible to say what would have happened at Calke if he had succeeded as 11th baronet. In the event Sir Vauncey was succeeded by his eldest daughter Hilda Ethelfreda Harpur Crewe who had married Colonel Mosley, a partner in the Derby firm of solicitors, Taylor, Simpson and Mosley, who had acted as solicitors to the family for many years.

Chapter Fifteen
Mrs. H. E. H. Mosley

FOLLOWING Sir Vauncey's death and the arrival of his successor, Calke took a small step into the 20th century. Horses and carriages were no longer to be seen on the drives and the motor car was at last allowed into the park. Mrs. Mosley had her own motor car and chauffeur, but although the carriages had become redundant she often drove round Ticknall and Calke in her pony and trap.

Mrs. Mosley shunned the limelight, preferring to live a life of comparative seclusion at Calke. From her great grandfather Sir George Crewe she inherited her strong sense of duty, guided by the highest moral Christian principles. She inherited the family estates, burdened by death duties and the depressed state of agriculture, together with the general state of disrepair into which the properties had fallen during her father's lifetime, when the emphasis had been on game preservation. A legacy of this was Calke Abbey crammed with his natural history collection, Sir Vauncey had left instructions that the collection must be kept in air conditioned rooms, but in the circumstances it was impossible to comply with his wishes. Shortly after his death part of the collection was sold so that what is now to be seen is only the residue of a lifetime's collecting. After this sale nothing in the house was disturbed again.

During my early days at the estate office, apart from my weekly visits to Calke to pay the staff wages, we had little to do with the day to day management of Calke Abbey and the gardens. Mrs. Mosley had her own establishment there. She had a minimum of domestic help in the house, and outside there was the farm bailiff in charge of the limited farming operations, a chauffeur, groom, joiner, a bricklayer and his man, a handyman and three gardeners. The men all worked well together and would do whatever was required to keep things going. There was no foreman. It could be said that Mrs. Mosley was herself in charge. She was a person who inspired loyalty, and everyone would go out of their way to please her.

In regard to repairs, the main task was to keep the Abbey and stables wind and watertight, and in this the estate office would be involved. If outside help was required, Barkers, the Melbourne plumbers, or Joseph Parker, an old established firm of builders in Derby would be called in, the only outside people entrusted with the care of the fabric of Calke. In the 1930s the stonework on the south front was showing serious signs of decay, and major repairs to the pilasters and the columns of the portico were necessary. Evidence of this work can still be seen.

Beyond the park walls, the management of the extensive farm and cottage properties, which were all let to tenants, was in the hands of Mr. Hooley as agent. Mr. Hooley who became agent in 1926 following the sudden death of Mr. Fuller, had been with the firm of Shaw & Fuller all his working life and was fully conversant with the family properties.

Opposite: Mrs Mosley.

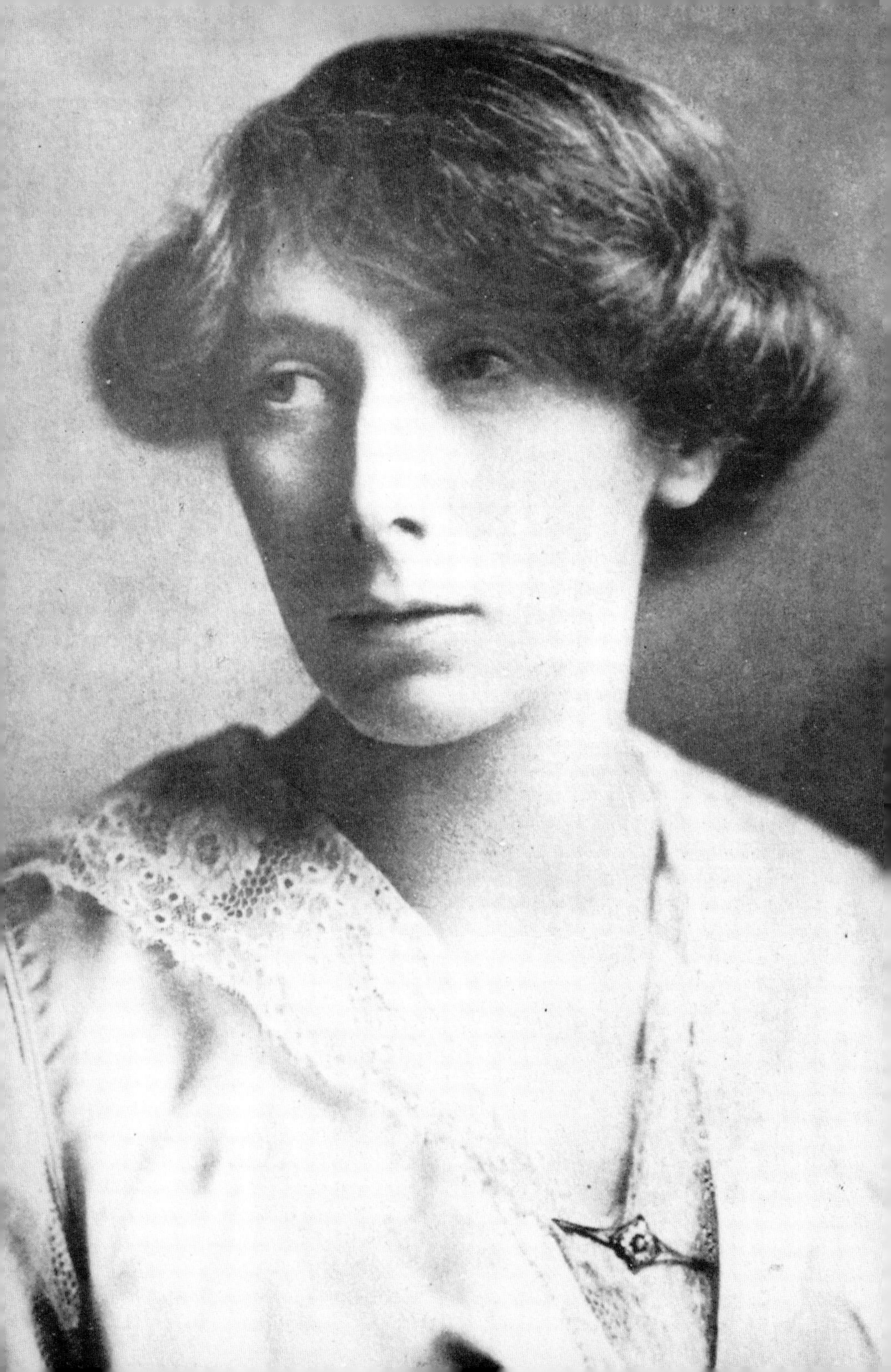

He would drive through the park to keep an eye on things and had regular meetings with Mrs. Mosley at Calke. She was on good terms with her agent and they shared an interest in roses. During the summer he always took roses with him when he called on her. On occasions when he was driving through the park and I was with him, he would send me to deliver the roses if he had no particular reason to call himself. Mrs. Mosley would often return the compliment by sending roses to Mr. & Mrs. Hooley from her own rose garden at Calke.

Through these regular visits, Mrs. Mosley would be kept informed about all that was happening on the estate and Mr. Hooley would give advice about matters requiring attention, and take her instructions. As the owner of a great landed estate she was like Sir George, far more concerned with her duties than with her rights, and the welfare of her numerous tenants was her primary concern. She expected to be kept informed about their circumstances, and was always ready to assist those in need. This she always did in her own quiet way, and in some cases only the persons concerned were aware of her interest and concern, and the practical help she gave.

Mrs. Mosley's husband, Colonel Mosley, was able, as a lawyer, to assist his wife in legal matters, but unfortunately did not see eye to eye with her agent in one important aspect of estate management. The whole estate was subject to the Settled Land Act which meant that the freehold was vested in Trustees, the legal title of the apparent owner Mrs. Mosley, being tenant for life. This meant that capital money vested in the trustees could not be used for repairs, which had to be paid for out of income. At one time the amount allowed by the tax authority to be spent on repairs and allowed against tax on income from property was strictly limited. When, however, the rule was changed so that the whole of maintenance could be set against tax, Mr. Hooley was anxious to take advantage of the new rule, to overcome the back-log of repairs on the estate. Colonel Mosley, however, advised against this on the grounds that a substantial increase in expenditure would lead tenants to expect this as a matter of course, if circumstances changed. For a time therefore, Mr. Hooley was restricted by this short-sighted view until the Colonel's death in 1945, when Mrs. Mosley agreed to what was obviously a more sensible course to follow. Unfortunately by then, a shortage of labour through many of the building workers being still away in the forces, together with a shortage of building materials and wartime building controls, prevented any real progress being made before Mrs. Mosley's untimely death in 1949, when the prospect of death duties called a halt to further progress at that time.

From 1924 to 1949 Mrs. Mosley lived quietly at Calke, her days fully occupied in looking after the great house. Although she lived a quiet, almost reclusive life at Calke, in this she was probably little different from many of her tenants, who lived in a similar way in their farmhouses and cottages.

She would occasionally invite friends to call but never entertained in the accepted sense of the word, apart from a rare occasion in 1938 when she entertained her tenants at a reception at Calke to mark the coming of age of the heir to the estates, her nephew Charles Jenney who, after her death was to become Charles Harpur Crewe. Her lifestyle was simple in the extreme. She never travelled far, but would sometimes accept invitations to open garden fetes and sales of work for charity, held in the neighbourhood.

She attended meetings of the Governors of Repton School, of which she was, as head of her family, an hereditary governor. She was patron of several livings in Derbyshire and Staffordshire and when a living became vacant would exercise great care when putting forward the name of a suitable candidate for the Bishop's approval.

When a farm became vacant she always liked to meet a prospective tenant recommended by her agent, and if possible visit him on his farm. This was in fact a fairly rare event because sons usually succeeded fathers, thus keeping farms in families, and vacant farms were usually offered to younger sons of tenants, who were looking for a farm of their own. When a farm was available for outside letting, however, such was the reputation of the Harpur Crewes as landlords that there was never any shortage of applicants.

The late John Gotheridge recalled the time when, as an outsider, he applied for the tenancy of Manor Farm, Smisby in 1936. One afternoon, he was working on his smallholding near Swadlincote, when his attention was drawn to two rather tramp-like figures, climbing over the roadside fence, and heading towards the farmhouse. The intruders proved to be Col. & Mrs. Mosley who had called to see them. Over a cup of tea, Mrs. Mosley told him that she would like him to take the tenancy, and that as the farm was in a run-down state, he could have it rent free for the first year. She wished him well, and said that if he had any problems he was to feel free to call at Calke Abbey to discuss them with her.

Mrs. Mosley was always happy to see any of her tenants who wished to call on her and regularly visited her tenants at Ticknall and Calke. In spite of a busy life she found time to take Sunday School for the children of Calke in a room in a cottage in the village.

Although in the possession of great wealth in terms of landed property and works of art, she had not the slightest interest in its monetary value. When the vet who attended her horses, admired the South American tooled leather saddle in the harness room and offered to purchase it she declined, even when he offered an open cheque.

Over the years, she earned the respect and affection, not only of her tenants, but of a wide circle beyond the boundaries of the estate. Her death in 1949 came as a great shock, news of her illness having been kept from all but those closest to her until it had taken a serious turn. The day after her death, I went as usual, on my cycle to Smisby to collect the weekly cottage rents, and found all the ladies except one in tears. The exception was Mrs. Fred Archer who was not given to tears, but said "With Mrs. Mosley's death, Smisby has lost the best friend it ever had."

On the morning of her funeral, I went to Calke with Mr. Hooley, who took with him, appropriately, a last bunch of roses from his garden as his personal tribute. At the Abbey we joined the small number of family mourners gathered in the entrance hall, and it was there that I met for the first time Charles Jenney, who had inherited the estates. The coffin, which had been made by the estate joiners from oak grown on the estate, was carried from the hall by employees acting as bearers, to be placed on the horse drawn farm dray which was waiting outside. From there, Mr. Hooley and I followed as George Topliss the farm bailiff led the horse on its sad journey along the drive, and up the hill to Calke Church where Mrs. Mosley's remains were to rest until the funeral later in the day. As I walked along in that procession I realised that this was the end of an era and nothing would ever be the same again. For me, the curtain had fallen on the world of the Harpur Crewes.

Chapter Sixteen
The Last Years

CHARLES HARPUR CREWE, who was then known as Charles Jenney, who succeeded, came into possession at the age of 31, totally unprepared for the position he had inherited.

That he did not visit Calke during the last years of his aunt's life can perhaps be understood, having regard to the differences between them, but it seems strange that he had made no attempt to prepare himself for the task that lay ahead. The Trustees must have been aware of the situation, but do not appear to have made any attempt to bridge the gap between Mrs. Mosley and her heir, or to suggest suitable training. As children, the Jenneys lived in Bedford where the brothers attended Bedford School. Neither boys showed scholastic ability, and did not go to college or university.

Charles came of age in 1938, and Mrs. Mosley gave a party at Calke to the tenants to mark the occasion. After this they grew apart, and appeared to have nothing in common. As a military man himself, Colonel Mosley persuaded Charles to join the army. It is said that he was reluctant to do so, but appears to have had nothing else in mind. He was commissioned in the Sherwood Foresters and spent part of the war in the Far East, something which he was always reluctant to talk of. After army service, he was for a short time a pupil on a farm in Somerset, but this did not lead to anything. Afterwards he appears to have done nothing in particular, partly because of an indolent nature, and perhaps because he knew he would never have to earn his living.

During my early years at the estate office, as far as I know, he visited Calke only once, and even then did not call on his aunt at the Abbey, where no doubt, he would not have been welcome anyway. He only got as far as to talk to the woodmen working in the park. He told them he had heard of me as Mr. Hooley's pupil, and wished to meet me. He was told that I could no doubt be found at the office, but did not call, and I did not meet him until the morning of Mrs. Mosley's funeral.

When his aunt died, he had no idea of the size of the estate and in fact, never did bring himself up-to-date with the details of his possessions.

Charles has been described as a recluse. He was not that, but was at times reclusive. If it had been otherwise, he would not have become Chairman of the South Derbyshire Conservative Association, or a member of the District Council. He took these positions, partly I think, because as head of the family he thought he ought to take part in public affairs, and partly because it gave him a reason to abdicate from his duties as owner of the estate, his interest in which was superficial, the management of which he did not understand, and made no effort to do so. Unfortunately, he lacked the knowledge or ability to take any meaningful part in public life in which he became involved. He never spoke in the various committees on which he served. He did, however, do a certain amount of work behind the scenes to help his constituents.

On the estate he would sometimes instigate misguided schemes and then unable to see them through, would panic, run away to hide, usually to Warslow or the town house in Bedford, and leave someone else to sort out the resulting muddle.

He was very economically minded. When he decided to plant an avenue of trees from the main gates to the front of the Abbey, he did not take advice or concern himself about suitable species. He simply looked round for the cheapest solution, and planted two rows of ash saplings which he had dug up in a nearby spinney. Their subsequent removal after his death need cause no regret.

He tended to be suspicious of everyone and trusted no one. I remember Mr. Hooley remarking to me one day on returning from a visit to Calke: "The trouble with Charles is that he treats everyone as his natural enemy". He was jealous of anyone who showed any ability that he himself did not possess, and would sometimes show this by becoming hostile, and behaving in an unfortunate way towards the person concerned. This no doubt stemmed from an inferiority complex.

Charles and his brother Henry differed from their aunt in so many ways and in one very important respect. Mrs. Mosley earned the respect in which she was held, whereas her nephews thought they were entitled to respect, because of who they were. An old friend of the family told me that both brothers suffered from an overdose of divine right!

During my time as assistant to Mr. Hooley, and afterwards to his successor, I got on reasonably well with Charles, mainly, I suppose, because I was not in a position to thwart his often misguided schemes. Mr. Preston resigned as agent in 1960 and I was appointed. He told me that he was leaving because Charles's lack of interest, in the estate, and his inability to make up his mind on anything, had driven him to despair. I was faced with a similar situation, but had been around long enough to understand.

Because I considered it his duty to visit all parts of the estate, I used to arrange half-yearly visits in March and September when he would accompany me to inspect work in progress and other matters of interest. He was always reluctant to do this, and I was able to arrange the date only with great difficulty. On the appointed day, we would begin in and around Ticknall, where he knew most of the tenants, and showed some interest. As we travelled on he would lose interest, and towards the end of the day would even refuse to leave the car to look at what I wanted him to see. He must have been very relieved when the day was over and I returned him to the Abbey.

Although this lack of interest in matters of importance and his inability to make decisions could be very frustrating, it did have its lighter moments.

As head of the family, he had the right to appoint vicars to various livings on the estate. Following a vacancy, he had six months to appoint, after which the right passed to the bishop. Charles's lack of knowledge and understanding of the situation made this difficult for him, and he always relied for help from his principal Trustee.

I remember one occasion, when the living of Repton was vacant, he came into the office and asked if he could hide for a while. When questioned, he told me he was running away from the Bishop of Derby, who was chasing him to make an appointment for Repton, about which he had not yet made up his mind. He went on to explain that, when the Bishop came in through the front door at Calke, he escaped by dodging out through the back. I ventured to suggest that this was no way to solve the problem, and in any case what would happen next. To this he replied "Oh, my sister is there, she will give him a cup of tea and a piece of cake, and when he is tired of waiting for me, he will go back to Derby." That was his way of putting off the evil day!

Charles Harpur Crewe with the Bishop of Derby the Rt. Revd. C. W. J. Bowles.

Each year came The Christmas Card Ritual, which always caused great amusement in the office. He expected to receive around eighty cards, and achieved this by sending out as many. Although frugal in his habits, and careful with money, he always had quite an expensive card printed, usually showing pheasants in a country scene. Each morning in the two weeks before Christmas, he would call at the office with his morning's post, and with the help of the office staff would dispatch cards to senders as they arrived. One year he decided that some of the cards he was receiving were not of the value he was sending, so he bought a large box of cheap cards at the local supermarket, with plenty of holly and robins, but with presumably, not too much about goodwill. These were then sent to those who had sent him a cheap card, and the staff would help him to value "suspect" incoming cards.

Most of his eccentricities caused amusement, but could sometimes lead to unfortunate consequences. One example of this, was the occasion, after I had left Calke, when he agreed to a request from his former agent, Christopher Preston, then living in retirement in Oxfordshire. The request was for a local arts and antiques society, of which he was secretary, to visit Calke to view the State Rooms.

On the appointed day, the party arrived by coach, only to find the house locked and the windows shuttered. Charles had left a message that he was involved with District Council elections in which he was a candidate, and it was not convenient for them to see the house, They could, however, have a picnic in the park.

Understandably this placed Mr. Preston in a very embarrassing position, and he had to try to placate some very irate members, who were not at all amused. In desperation, he telephoned his old friend, Mrs. Andrew Kerr, at nearby Melbourne Hall, who came to the rescue. She knew Charles well, and what he was capable of. She invited the party to Melbourne to view the Hall, and afterwards entertained them to a splendid tea, as she said "By way of compensation for being to badly treated".

In character, I found Charles both simple and complicated. We had hardly anything in common. As the years went by, my life became increasingly difficult and without a loyal staff would have found it impossible. His lack of interest in the estate, and in what I was trying to achieve, meant that I had to make my own decisions. based on the Harpur Crewe tradition, although this rarely found favour. One day, when I ventured to criticise something he had done, and remarked that Mrs. Mosley would not have acted in that way, he replied "There is no point in talking like that. We all know Aunt Hilda was a saint, and I camot be expected to live up to that".

Neither Charles nor his brother would take advice from those qualified to give it, but would listen to so-called friends, who usually gave advice in their own interest. In the end, I found it difficult to work with him to the point of impossibility. I left Calke in 1970, but continued to manage the family's property in the village of Breadsall, north of Derby. It was some years before we established a good relationship again.

One day, early in 1979, I received a telephone call from Calke Abbey in the form of an s.o.s., and he asked me to meet him there. In the panelled 'Swarkeston' room, he explained that re-organisation of the South Derbyshire District Council had left him without a partner, to stand for the two joint seats in the Ticknall Ward, involving six villages, in the forthcoming election. I had not been a councillor for twelve years, but several glasses of sherry later, I agreed, provided I ran as an independent, as I had always done. He would of course stand as a conservative. On one occasion he remarked with a laugh 'I can't stand these independents. You never know which way they are going to jump!'

The ensuing successful election campaign caused much amusement to all concerned, and is a story in itself. We sat together in Council and on most committees, but he never spoke. If anything under discussion concerned us, and was not going the way we might have wished, he would nudge me and whisper: 'We cannot allow them to get away with that. Get up and tell them!' whereupon I would do my best to oblige.

Sadly Charles died suddenly in 1981. He was living alone at Calke and collapsed in the park. It is thought he was hurrying home to avoid a thunderstorm. In accordance with his wish, he was buried, not in the family vault, but in the churchyard at Calke.

His life is best summed up by Christopher Preston, his former agent, who in a letter to me wrote. 'Poor Charles. He inherited so much but achieved so little'.

Following the death of Charles, his brother succeeded as Henry Jenney, but shortly afterwards, he and his sister Airmyne assumed the name of Harpur Crewe.

He inherited at a time of crisis, with crippling capital tax demands, causing grave doubts about the future of Calke Abbey. It was unfortunate that at this time, Henry, who had always been jealous of his brother, wishing to make his mark as head of the family, decided to take up the highly speculative and expensive hobby of horse racing, something of which he had no knowledge, and previously, no real interest. Before this, I saw him on horseback only once, and then he looked as if he was about to fall off! It seemed that, determined to make his mark at Calke, and having no ideas of his own, he sought to imitate his ancestor Sir Harry, the 6th baronet, and in fact, adopted his racing colours. At the time, I suggested that if he was looking for a role model it would be better for all concerned, if he modelled himself on his far more illustrious ancestor, Sir George Crewe, and could make a start by reading his diaries. This did not appeal to him at all, and he dismissed the suggestion, telling me that in any case, he could not read Sir George's handwriting! Sir George regarded horse racing as a menace.

After this, racing became an obsession, and was an acute embarrassment to the Trustees, who were struggling to pay enormous capital transfer tax and trying to secure the future of Calke Abbey.

Following family tradition, in 1991, he served as High Sheriff for Derbyshire, but died suddenly during his term of office. I was present at his funeral at Calke, and assisted at the interment in the family vault. I entered the vault for the first time, the day before the funeral, and descending the steps, the first coffin I saw ahead of me was that of Sir John. I recognised this, because it was of oak, with heavy silver gilt fittings, exactly as described by Henry Forman who attended the funeral in 1886. It was so well preserved, and looked as if it had been placed there only the day before. Looking further, I located Sir George's coffin, covered with brass studded leather, and nearby that of his beloved grandmother, Lady Frances Harpur, whose portrait dominates the saloon at Calke. It was a strange feeling to be so close to the mortal remains of members of the family I had learned to respect. I was greatly moved, and began to understand how relics came to be venerated.

Following Henry's death, Airmyne succeeded, who had lived at Warslow Hall, on the North Staffordshire Estate, since the death of Charles in 1981. She told me she never expected to outlive Henry, and faced her unexpected inheritance and its problems with courage. In character she was very different from her brothers. She was intelligent, kind, considerate and generous, and always looked for the best in people. No one visited her without coming away with a gift of some kind. Naturally shy, she was also physically handicapped. During the last war, she served at the remount stables at Melton Mowbray, where serious injuries following an accident with a horse left her with a speech impediment. In spite of this she never lost her love of horses, and two of her favourites spent their last years at Calke. In later years she suffered from arthritis, which made walking difficult, and she found it difficult to write the numerous letters she liked to send. Ever mindful of her tenants, particularly those in ill-health or distress, I likened her to Mrs. Mosley, her aunt, and to Lady Crewe, her grandmother. Her death in 1999 brought to an end the long line of Harpurs and Harpur Crewes, in direct descent from Sir Henry Harpur, the first baronet, who arrived at Calke in 1622. She was buried at Calke, when the family vault was opened again for the last time.

I consider it unfortunate that, on Mrs. Mosley's death, Airmyne could not have succeeded, ahead of her brothers. If she had done so, I am sure I would have had a different story to tell of Calke's later years.

Chapter Seventeen
Postscript

MANY years have passed by since I stood in Twyford Schoolyard looking towards the Formark Hills and wondering what lay beyond. Much of this book describes what I found there. In it I have written of a world which has gone beyond recall except through memory. It is perhaps all too easy to look back through rose coloured spectacles to a golden age which some would say never really existed, but I can recall through my own memory, and the memories of my family and others, nearly 150 years of the Harpur Crewes at Calke, and the tradition they established. I have respect for that tradition of benevolent land ownership, founded by Sir George Crewe in the first half of the nineteenth century and carried on by succeeding generations of the family, assisted to the best of their ability by their land agents. I feel privileged to have been part of that succession and tradition. The family's concern for the land and the interests and welfare of their tenants was paramount. This may be derided by some as feudal or paternalistic, but it was a good deal more humane and effective than some aspects of the modern welfare state, overburdened by a costly and often inefficient administration. I know because I was there and was involved.

Calke Abbey has now entered a new era, and the story of how it was saved for the nation after being so nearly lost has been told elsewhere. I was invited to Calke in September 1984 when the Duchess of Devonshire launched the National Trust's Calke Abbey Appeal in a marquee in front of the house. Closing my eyes for a moment while the Duchess was speaking, I thought how different the occasion might have been. Instead of Her Grace, there could well have been an auctioneer from one of the country's leading firms, selling off the contents of Calke lot by lot, before a company of dealers and collectors and the idly curious, to be dispersed for ever.

However, on that day in October 1985 when Calke Park was opened to the public for the first time, I must confess that, as I drove along the lime tree avenue from Ticknall, a road I had travelled so many times before, and saw the visitors there, I felt somewhat resentful that everyone could now go where before only the privileged few had been permitted. For this I hope I may be forgiven.

Whatever their faults and failings, whatever their eccentricities. the Harpur Crewes did not deserve to be treated by the Treasury as they have been in the recent past. They lived quietly at Calke, surrounded by their tenants paying moderate rents, undisturbed in their farms and cottages.

The Harpur Crewes were bound by a strict family settlement, designed to preserve the estate intact, but which unfortunately had the opposite effect. The ownership was vested in trustees and the apparent owners of Calke were only tenants for life, although on death they were treated for capital tax as though they were absolute owners. The terms of the settlement were so strict that neither trustees nor tenant for life had any room for manoeuvre in regard to tax avoidance. Thus the estate was a sitting target for the Treasury when death occurred. It seems ironic that the only serious mistake the

Henry Harpur-Crewe with the Duchess of Devonshire at the launching of the Calke Abbey Appeal in September 1984.

owners of Calke made was to die, which unleashed the fury of the taxman.

In this way, I have seen the family property diminish over the years from 10,000 acres in Derbyshire and Leicestershire and 25,000 acres in North Staffordshire to, by comparison, a mere handful of acres today. Only the transfer of Calke Abbey, with Calke village and the central core of the Derbyshire estate to the National Trust, has prevented total disaster.

In this book I have written as much about the tenants as about their landlords. This was inevitable because their lives were bound together. During my time large parts of the estate have been broken up. There are now many new faces. All those I knew when I first arrived at Calke have gone, and I am now a late lingerer on the scene. With the new faces have come new ideas, many alien to the Harpur Crewe tradition as I knew it. Much of the natural order of things has been replaced by sophistication. Sophistication, like the curate's egg, is good in parts, but does not have a lot in its favour.

Appendix

Mr. & Mrs. Vauncey Crewe's visit to the lakes

IN 1876, the year of their marriage, Mr. & Mrs. Vauncey Crewe, as they then were, spent two weeks touring in the English Lakes, and Mrs. Crewe wrote a diary in which she describes the places they visited.

Accompanied by her maid, Elizabeth Castle, they travelled by train from Derby to Grange-over-Sands, and then by coach, open carriage, waggonette and pony and trap to see places of interest now well known to today's tourists. Vauncey bought ferns in Ambleside, and nearby "searched for a butterfly he was in want of, but without success". She described in detail the journey to see Wastwater Lake. "It is most difficult to reach". At Seathwaite the carriage could go no further. so they took out the horse, put a side saddle on for Mrs. Crewe to ride, Vauncey walking by the side. Five miles on, they reached Wasdale, where they took lunch, and then both had to walk the last mile to the lake, which she described as a "very dismal spot".

They visited the Borrowdale Pencil Works, and then, near Penrith, drove to see what Mrs. Crewe described as a "Druidicle Circle" a fine circle comes next to Stonehenge. We met a very cross man there, who would not let us walk round it as he said the place belonged to him, and we spoilt his grass. He became very rude and was quite insulting, so we drove back again to Penrith". It is amusing to read this, when one recalls that in later years, after Vauncey inherited from his father, much time was spent ordering trespassers off his thousands of acres!

On the journey home, they called at Carlisle and Durham, where they visited both cathedrals, which she describes in some detail. In Carlisle they were shown round by a nice old verger. The organ was being enlarged, which the verger thought unnecessary as he said it was quite loud enough before, and would bring the tower down, the foundations of which had already given way a little. Durham Cathedral was undergoing restoration, so they could not see the "fine architecture to advantage" but she noted: "The choir is very good and is the highest paid one in England". The city itself seemed to her a "bad place, with a great deal of drunkenness", which she attributed to the collieries.

On returning to Calke, they were met at Ticknall Lodge by the pupils of Lady Crewe's school, assembled outside to sing a song of welcome, accompanied by a harmonium. Mrs. Marriott of Ticknall, who as Rosa Shreeve, was the smallest pupil, recalled climbing on top of the harmonium to obtain a better view. After listening to the pupils, the couple proceeded to Calke Abbey, along the lime tree avenue planted in 1846 to mark Vauncey's birth.

This poem, written by Hannah Hudson in 1879 recalls the death by drowning in 1840 in one of the ponds in Calke Park of William Hudson (son of John Hudson, gamekeeper to Sir George Crewe) and his friend John Atkin (son of William Atkin, the Ticknall clockmaker). William Hudson was Hannah Hudson's uncle. Both boys were fifteen years of age and they were buried together in a corner of Ticknall churchyard were their grave can still be seen. The story of the tragedy was told to Hannah Hudson by the boy's mother, Hannah's grandmother. The master referred to in the poem was Sir George Crewe, who organised the search for the missing boys

THE LOST ONES

Tis winter and within that Keeper's home
As clean as woman's hands can make the place
Anxiously a Mother's waiting for her son
She's waited long, and still he does not come.

"Where can he be, I wonder. I will clear
The breakfast things when surely he'll be here".
She clears the table, washes up, then lays the
    cloth again
"I'll set his breakfast ready, he'll surely be here
    then"
Then going to the window, again she strained her
    eyes
And while she looks, a little bird into the cottage
    flies,
And lighted on the waiting cup and dropped in
    dead
And sad forebodings soon begin to fill the
    Mother's head,
And as the father enters in the cottage door
She says "I think I never shall see William any
    more
For this little robin in his cup just tumbled o'er and
    died
Put on your hat and go and look for him" the
    mother cried.

THE SEARCH

The father seized his hat, and goes out to meet
Ah! little does he think how many miles his feet
Shall walk before his search shall sadly end.
He goes to where his son works with his friend
"I say, have you seen anything of my son?"
"Yes he was here this morn, but he is to his
    breakfast gone".
"Ah, but he's never reached. where is his mate?"
"I'll go for him for it is getting late".
"Gone home." "Then I will hasten off to see if he
    is there".
"But no", said they", he never has been here
And more than that, our boy is missing too
Wherever are they gone?"

He now resumes the anxious winter search
Out set the fathers now of both the lads
Of everyone they meet they both enquire
"Oh, have you seen anything of my son?"
Each of them treads his separate weary way
And all their friends are on the sad look out
    For tidings of the lost.
The father searches all the country round
Both far and near, and strains his eager eyes
And ever and anon bursts forth the cry.
"William, my son, my son, where art thou gone
I know not whither I must go to next
Art thou my son for ever from me gone
Has hungry death made thee his prey
Or art thou 'neath the icy surface of the pond.
I see no mark of broken ice, I've looked all round
Or art thou tired of thy humble home
And gone away without a farewell word?
Answer my son, and I will pardon all"
But oh! no answer comes.

"The night is coming on again, and I
Must go back home and meet thy mother's face
And then her piercing look of dread despair
Her bitter wail of woe, alas, my son
My sorrow is too hard for me to bear
This dread suspense, this mingled hope and fear
These longing eyes, this breathless listening
These parched lips, this burning throbbing brow
Can bear the winter's blast upon it now
And feel no cold, nor can I swallow food
And thy poor mother's face is more than I can bear".

"William, my son, my son, oh speak to me.
Eight days have passed since I saw thy face
Beaming with manhood's pride, yet boyhood's
    grace.
Thy sunny looks, they tender bright blue eyes

They stalwart form, thou wert the joy, my son
Of all the younger children, and the pride
Of all the older ones".

"Dearer thou seemst to me than all the rest
Because that thou art gone, I know not where
I dare not hope to see thy face again
Nor dare I utter what I now most fear
That thou art drowned.
I would to God, my son, that thou were found".

They meet again, the parents of the boy,
But neither dares to speak one word of hope
But as they look into each other's face
They read the sad, sad tale
No tidings of the lost. No, not one word.

And so they sit them down beside the fire
To rest and try to take a little food
But they are full already, full of grief, but they
  must try
Just for the sake of those who are left
For working men must work, though sorrows press
And weary limbs must rest, but as for sleep
The poor gamekeeper cannot think of that
But dozes now and then, and in his dreams
He sees his missing son and tries to speak
And take him to his breast. But no
He wakes up, and lo, 'tis but a dream.

The mother sits besides the lowering fire
With head bowed down and buried in her hands
Breathlessly listening, for oh the faintest sound
Of footsteps would drive the dark despair
From off that mother's face.

But still no sound save that the cruel wind
Drives in through all the crevices around
And makes her shiver with the piercing cold.
Then up she starts, and reaching for a light
Upon the cottage mantel-piece she sees
Some rude carved toys in shape of man and horse
Or birds, or anything that took his fancy
Which he has made to try and please the little ones.
She takes one down and presses to her lips
Because her boy had touched, yea and formed
Not for the world would she exchange those toys
Not for the grandest carving ever done, oh no.

She puts it back and sadly climbs the stairs
And takes her light to look at all the little ones
But they have lost their charm since he is gone.
She turns away and fain would burst in tears
But they are all dried up. "Oh where's my boy?
My darling could I speak to thee again

"T'would ease this choking pain that fills my throat
William, my darling boy" she groans, "My boy".

The lays her down beside her sorrowing husband
But neither speak, t'would only add to sorrow
Their hope is gone for him, he must be dead.
For he was not a thoughtless youth.
And would not keep them eight days in suspense
And now 'twas nearly nine.

The morning comes, the piercing bitter wind
Blows bleak. but in that father's heart
Affection deep is burning for his son
He takes his gun, and treads his way to work
And meets his master who the day before
Had said "No matter what it costs
Tomorrow I will have the fishponds dragged
The men shall break the ice and boat it off
I can no longer bear to see thy haggard face
For it is better far to know the worst
Than to live on a life of dread suspense."

FOUND

So in the morning as they meet, the master knows
He had not found his son, for were it thus
He now would raise his head and meet him with a
  smile
So without opening afresh the wound
By asking needless questions
He commands the men to break the ice
On that pond first into which the drainage
Down from the Abbey runs.

The men work hard for they all loved the youth
And pitied the poor father whose sad look
Called forth their utmost sympathy
The father stands beside the pond in dread
With clenched hands and downcast head, but now
He raised his eyes and looked upon the men
As if in some strange dream.
The master looking on in eager dread
Fearing for the poor father
And now the pond, at length, is clear of ice
They fetch the drags, the master nears the father's
  side
Trembling with fear, and yet a gleam of hope
Would linger in his eye, the boy might not be there.
So now they put the drag in where the drainage runs
For there the ice would be the shallowest
If they had gone to slide.
They gently draw it out, and lo, what is it comes?
  A hat.

A wild despairing cry bursts from the father
William, my own dear son, is drowned, is
   drowned".
His master gently drew him from the spot
Come home with me, John. 'tis no sight for thee
It is enough to know that he is dead
Without the pain of seeing his body dragged
That is too much for thee.
Get in the carriage, come along with me
And we will take the tidings to his mother
Remember, John, thou sufferest not alone
His friend has parents too, as dear as he".

So off they go to tell the waiting mother
Who, though bowed down with sorrow, not
   surprised
But said "I knew, ah yes, I knew it all
For when I saw that little robin fall
Into his cup, I knew I ne'er should see
My boy alive again".
And when they bear the precious burden home
The mother wipes his dripping, sodden face
And brushes back the sunny locks, and scarce
Believes that he will never wake again
The bright blue eyes are open wide
The colour in his cheeks is fresh, but oh, the life is
   gone
He must be buried soon, he has been dead nine
   days.

And now the funeral sadly moves along
They take them to the sheltered quiet corner
And bury them side by side, and write
Upon their tombstone their sad tale,
Lest they should ever be forgot
But ah, that mother never will forget
I've heard her tell the tale so many times
And seen the tears run down her aged cheeks
Though when it happened she was young
   compared
To what her age is now.
And oh, shall e'er that father's heart forget
That dreadful search for his beloved son?
Forget! The anguish that then filled his breast
Or how he loved the one he could not find
Or his despair when he had found him dead.
No Never.

Hannah Hudson 1st February 1879
In manus Tuas, Domine, commendo spiritum meum

Document appointing John Hudson as Gamekeeper of Calke Abbey.

To all to whom these Presents shall come I Sir Vauncey Harpur Crewe of Calke Abbey in the County of Derby Baronet Lord of the Manors of Barrow upon Trent, Alvaston and Boulton, Swarkestone, Stanton by Bridge, Sinfin, Stenson, Arleston, Pollock, Findern, Twyford, Calke, Ticknall, Repton, Smisby and Chellaston all in the County of Derby **Send Greeting** **Know ye** that I the said Sir Vauncey Harpur Crewe do hereby appoint authorise constitute and empower **John Hudson** of Twyford in the said County of Derby to be a Gamekeeper of and in all and every my Manors of Barrow upon Trent, Alvaston and Boulton, Swarkestone, Stanton by Bridge, Sinfin, Stenson, Arleston, Pollock, Findern, Twyford, Calke, Ticknall, Repton, Smisby and Chellaston and all the royalties rights members and appurtenances to them or any of them belonging during my pleasure with full power license and authority within and upon my said Manors and every of them to kill any hare, pheasant, partridge, grouse or any other game whatever for my sole use and benefit **And also** to keep and preserve the game within all and every the said Manors **And** for the purpose of enabling the said John Hudson to preserve within the said Manors I give and grant unto him my pleasure full power and authority to take and seize all such greyhounds setting dogs lurchers ferrets trammells lowbells hayes harepipes snares gins or other engines for the taking and killing of pheasants partridges moor game as within the precincts of the said Manors shall be in the possession or custody of any person or persons who by the laws of this realm are prohibited to keep the same **And** I the said Sir Vauncey Harpur Crewe do hereby authorise impower and empower the said John Hudson to seize detain and keep all and every net angle rod or other engine which he shall find set or laid in or in the custody of any person or persons in or upon any river brook or streams within any of my Manors without my consent **And** I do also give and grant unto the said John Hudson full power and authority to do every other act and thing requisite to authorise as being for the preservation of the game within and every the said Manors and for the discovering and conviction of the offenders in the destruction and pursuit of the game against the laws and statutes of this realm **In witness** whereof I have hereunto subscribed my name and affixed my seal this twenty sixth day of February One thousand eight hundred and eighty eight nine —

Signed sealed and delivered
by the above named Sir
Vauncey Harpur Crewe in the
presence of

V. H. Crewe

John Shaw

About the Author

Leslie John Cox is a chartered surveyor who was born at Twyford in South Derbyshire, one of the outlying villages on the Calke Abbey estate. He was educated at the village school at Twyford and Bemrose School, Derby.

He began his professional career as a pupil in the Calke Abbey Estate Office at Ticknall, later becoming assistant agent. During this time he graduated in estate management at London University as an external student.

In 1956 he succeeded to the firm of Shaw & Fuller, agent to the estate for over 100 years. He was agent at Calke from 1960-69.

In 1979 he was elected with Charles Harpur-Crewe to the South Derbyshire District Council where he served as a member for the Ticknall Ward.

In 1983, when the future of Calke Abbey was in doubt from the burden of Capital Transfer Tax, following the death of Charles Harpur-Crewe, Councillor Cox brought the problems faced by Henry Harpur-Crewe and his Trustees in their efforts to secure the future of Calke, to the attention of the South Derbyshire District Council. After consultation with the Trustees, the Council promoted a campaign to save Calke and enlisted the support of neighbouring District and County Councils. Intervention of these authorities played an important part in the campaign to preserve Calke for the nation.